PHYSICS
GCSE Grade Booster

J. J. Brennan

Schofield & Sims Ltd.

0 7217 4615 2

First printed 1989

To my father, Joseph Brennan, who inspired,
encouraged and motivated my career in the
very beautiful world of Physics.

J.J.B.

Schofield & Sims Ltd.
Dogley Mill
Fenay Bridge
Huddersfield
HD8 0NQ
England

Designed by Ocean Typesetting, Leeds
Printed in England by Alden Press

Contents

Introduction

This Physics Grade Booster is written to help you revise in the last part of your GCSE course. It is not intended as a textbook and you should use a text and/or your notes to check details. You should also read your syllabus to see if there are any sections you can omit.

The book is arranged in such a way that it will be convenient for revision. Throughout you will find headings and subheadings in the margin, with definitions, explanations, equations, examples, etc., to the right of the margin. Use a card with the book to expose the keyword in the margin, but keep the right-hand side covered. Then try to recall the material on the right. By careful lowering of the card, you can allow yourself to see just enough of the writing to prompt you.

Acknowledgements

Grateful acknowledgement is due to Dr. Peter Fryer of Bradford and Ilkley Community College, who originated the format and is the author of the companion volume on Chemistry; to Mr. Bill Ross, also of B.I.C.C., who kindly read and made suggestions for improvements in the first draft; and to Mrs. Halina Reid, who typed the manuscript with remarkable patience and skill. Special thanks are due to Dr. Martin Dickinson of Humberside College for a very careful reading of the final draft.

J. J. Brennan

Symbols

To save space the following notation has been adopted:
- $\sim$ denotes 'of the order of', i.e. to the nearest power of ten.
- $\simeq$ denotes 'is approximately equal to'.
- $=$ denotes 'is equal to'.
- $>$ denotes 'is greater than'.
- $<$ denotes 'is less than'.
- $\therefore$ denotes 'therefore'.
- $\propto$ denotes 'varies directly as'.

1 Atomic Structure

Atom	An atom is the smallest part of an element that can take part in a *chemical* reaction. An atom has a diameter $\sim 10^{-10}$ m. All atoms consist of a central core having a diameter $\sim 10^{-14}$ m. Hence, most of an atom consists of empty space.
Nucleus	The nucleus is the central core of an atom. Nearly all of the mass of an atom is concentrated in the nucleus.
Nucleon	A nucleon is the collective name for the two types of particle that exist in the nucleus. The nucleus is positively charged.
Proton (p)	A proton is the particle contributing to the positive charge in the core. The mass of a proton, $m_p \simeq 1.7 \times 10^{-27}$ kg.
Neutron (n)	A neutron is the second type of particle existing in the nucleus. It has a mass m_n almost identical to the mass of a proton and is uncharged: $m_n \simeq m_p$.
Electron (e)	An electron is a negatively charged particle which orbits the nucleus at a definite distance from it. The *size* of the charge associated with an electron is the same as that of the proton but opposite in sign. The mass of an electron, $m_e \simeq \dfrac{1}{2000} m_p$.
Electron Shell	Several electrons circulating at approximately the same distance from the nucleus constitute an electron shell.
Ion	If electrons are added to or subtracted from an electrically neutral atom (i.e. an atom where the number of electrons and protons is equal), what is left is called an ion. An ion with a deficit of electrons will be positively charged, and one with an excess of electrons will be negatively charged.
Ionisation	Ionisation is the process of forming ions.
Proton Number or Atomic Number (Z)	The proton number is the number of protons in the nucleus. In a neutral atom it is also the number of orbiting electrons. It is given the symbol Z. The number of orbiting electrons dictates the chemical properties of the atom and thus fixes the location of an element in the Periodic Table.
Neutron Number (N)	The neutron number is the number of neutrons in the nucleus. It is given the symbol N.
Mass Number (A)	The mass number is the number of nucleons in the nucleus (i.e. the number of protons plus neutrons). It is given the symbol A.

5

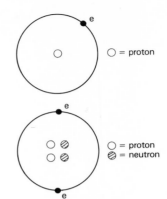

Hydrogen Atom	A hydrogen atom comprises a single proton constituting the nucleus and a single orbiting electron. There are no neutrons. This is the lightest atom known.

Helium Atom	A helium atom comprises four nucleons (2 protons and 2 neutrons) and two orbiting electrons.

Alpha Particle An alpha particle is a doubly ionised helium atom – that is, a helium atom minus the two orbiting electrons, i.e. a helium nucleus.

Symbolic Notation for Atomic Nuclei An atom X would be labelled $_Z^A X$.

The hydrogen atom would be labelled $_1^1 H$; and the helium atom, $_2^4 He$. The table below shows the particles in some typical atoms.

Element	Hydrogen	Helium	Iron	Silver	Gold	Lead	Uranium
Protons	1	2	26	47	79	82	92
Neutrons	0	2	30	60	116	126	146
Electrons	1	2	26	47	79	82	92
Notation	$_1^1 H$	$_2^4 He$	$_{26}^{56} Fe$	$_{47}^{107} Ag$	$_{79}^{195} Au$	$_{82}^{208} Pb$	$_{92}^{238} U$

Nuclide A nuclide is an atom with a specified value of Z and A; $_Z^A X$.

Alternative Notation Sometimes it is convenient to specify a nuclide by its mass number only, e.g. U-235.

Isotopes Nuclides with the same atomic number Z – different atoms of the same element having different numbers of neutrons in the nucleus (i.e. different A) – are called isotopes of that element. Isotopes of an element have the same chemical properties. There are two further types of hydrogen, labelled deuterium and tritium ($_1^2 H$ and $_1^3 H$, respectively).

The nucleus of deuterium comprises 1 p and 1 n. Similarly the nucleus of tritium comprises 1 p and 2 n. Both have only one orbiting electron.

Heavy Water Water made from deuterium is called heavy water and has a density of over 1100 kg/m^3.

2 Radioactivity

Radioactivity Radioactivity is the spontaneous disintegration of certain unstable types of atomic nuclei by the emission of alpha (α) particles or beta (β) particles and sometimes gamma (γ) rays. Both α and β decay alter the chemical nature of the atom as a result of the change in atomic number and the end product is usually a more stable nucleus. Any excess energy possessed by the nucleus after α or β emission is emitted in the form of a γ ray photon. A photon, loosely, is a packet of energy.

α Particles Alpha particles are double ionised helium atoms, i.e. an He atom minus the two normally orbiting electrons. They consist of 2p and 2n and are *positively charged.*

Properties of α Particles
1. Low penetrating power. They travel about 3-4 cm in air and can be stopped by a sheet of paper.
2. High speeds $\sim 10^7$ m/s.
3. Deflected by a magnetic field.
4. Capable of strong ionisation of gases.
5. Very intense over short distances.
6. Do not penetrate skin.

β Particles Beta particles are high energy electrons. They originate in the nucleus (see β Decay).

Properties of β Particles
1. Intermediate penetrating power. They travel about 1 m in air and can be stopped by a thin sheet of aluminium or clothing.
2. High speeds – they can travel at speeds approaching that of light in air (3×10^8 m/s).
3. Deflected by a weak magnetic field. (The mass of a beta particle is about $\dfrac{1}{8000}$ that of an alpha particle.)
   A β particle will be deflected in the opposite direction to that of an α particle.
4. Capable of ionisation intermediate between α particles and γ rays.
5. Less intense than α particles.
6. Can penetrate skin to reach sensitive body tissues.

γ Rays Gamma rays originate in the nucleus. They are electromagnetic waves of very short wavelength.

Properties of γ Rays
1. Extremely penetrating. They can travel several hundred metres in air and can penetrate the whole body.
   Lead attenuates very effectively the propagation of γ rays but does not stop them completely.

2. Travel at the speed of light in a vacuum.
3. Not deflected by a magnetic field.
4. Produce weak ionisation of gases.
5. Less intense than β particles.

Disintegration Rate or Activity

The disintegration rate is the number of disintegrations per second. It is directly proportional to the number of undecayed nuclei present in a radioactive element (a radioisotope) and is independent of external factors such as temperature or pressure.

Cosmic Rays

Cosmic rays are energetic particles reaching the Earth from space consisting mainly of protons with smaller amounts of heavier nuclei. They are affected by the Earth's magnetic field. More rays enter at the poles than at the equator.

Background Radiation

Background radiation is low intensity radiation arising from cosmic rays and the presence of naturally occurring radioisotopes in rocks, building materials, soil and air. Human beings are also slightly radioactive as a consequence of taking in radioactive nuclides present in food. C-14 occurs in plants. Ra-226 and Th-232 are sometimes present in food and water. K-40 is present in milk, cheese and potatoes. Nuts are relatively highly radioactive.

Radon and Thoron

Radon and thoron are radioactive gases given off from certain types of rock. They tend to concentrate inside buildings. They disperse effectively in the outside environment.

Half-Life ($T_{\frac{1}{2}}$)

Half-life is the time taken for the activity of a radioisotope to decay to half of its original value. Symbol $T_{\frac{1}{2}}$. Half-lives of different substances vary over a very wide range from less than a millionth of a second to more than a million years, e.g. polonium-212 has a half-life of 3×10^{-7} s whilst uranium-235 has a half-life of 7×10^8 years.

Geiger Muller (G.M.) Tube

A Geiger Muller tube is an instrument capable of detecting ionising radiations (α, β and γ rays).

Scaler

A scaler is a counting device. It produces an output pulse when an input pulse (or pulses) has been received. When used in conjunction with a G.M. tube, events taking place in the tube can be counted. An event entails an α or β particle or γ ray ionising a gas atom in the tube. The rate at which events take place gives a measure of the strength of a monitored radioactive source. We must be careful to correct the apparent count-rate of a source for 'background'.

Ratemeter

A ratemeter is an electronic device which, when connected to a G.M. tube, provides us with an average count-rate. Again when monitoring a radioactive source the average count-rate associated with background radiation must be subtracted in order to obtain the average count-rate from the source at any particular time.

Experiment to Obtain the Half-Life of a Radioisotope

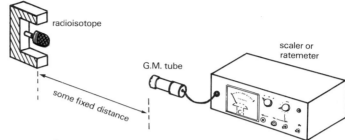

radioisotope

scaler or ratemeter

G.M. tube

some fixed distance

Typical Tabulation of Results

Intensity of source is directly proportional to the count-rate at a given time. Monitor the count-rate over a few hours.

Count-rate per minute	470	270	170	120	95	82
Time in hours	0	1	2	3	4	5

Typical Graphical Presentation

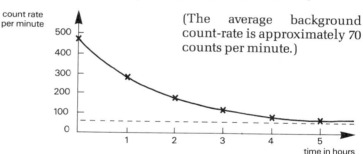

(The average background count-rate is approximately 70 counts per minute.)

Corrected count-rate per minute	400	200	100	50	25	12
Time in hours	0	1	2	3	4	5

Analysis

The half-life of the source in question is one hour, since every hour the count rate (i.e. the activity) halves. Bismuth-212, for example, has a half-life of one hour.

Radioactive Decay Processes

With the exception of hydrogen all naturally occurring nuclei consist of more than one nucleon. The ratio of neutrons to protons increases from 1:1 for the lightest nuclei to nearly 1.6:1 for the heaviest nuclei.

All nuclei with $A > 208$ are unstable to some extent, and no nuclei > 238 occur in nature.

α Decay

α decay: $\quad {}^{A}_{Z}X \longrightarrow {}^{A-4}_{Z-2}Y + {}^{4}_{2}\alpha$

e.g. $\quad\quad {}^{238}_{92}U \longrightarrow {}^{234}_{90}Th + {}^{4}_{2}\alpha$

9

β Decay   Nuclei which have too many neutrons emit β particles. A neutron changes into a proton and generates a β particle.

β decay: $_Z^A X \rightarrow\ _{Z+1}^{A} Y\ +\ \beta$

e.g. $_{49}^{116} In \rightarrow\ _{50}^{116} Sn\ +\ _{-1}^{0}\beta$

These β particles should *not* be confused with electrons which originate from the electron shells surrounding the nucleus. β particles are much more energetic than the electrons from the shells.

Nuclear Configuration   Just as electrons can spin only in certain permitted shells so the nucleons in a nucleus are arranged in certain permitted configurations. After most nuclear transitions the nucleus remains in an *excited state*. The nucleus rearranges itself to form the optimum configuration and in doing so emits γ rays. This optimum configuration is sometimes called the *ground state*.

Hazards Associated with Radioactive Emission   The effects of external β radiation are mainly confined to the body surface. Protective clothing can provide virtually complete shielding against β radiation. The greatest hazard with β emitting isotopes is when they are ingested in food or water or inhaled into the lungs. α particles are about 8000 times as massive as β particles, and have a double positive charge. Again they are a hazard only if taken into the body but can be much more damaging than β particles. However, we all have measurable quantities of α emitters inside us. The source is radon emanating from the Earth, decaying into Po-210 which finishes up in our food and drinking water.

Neutrons are capable of being absorbed in another nucleus and β particles or γ rays (and to a lesser degree α particles) are emitted as by-products.

X-rays and γ rays are extremely penetrating and cause the least damage per unit of distance travelled, but they penetrate further into the body. β radiation, X-rays and γ rays can cause radiation burns.

Safety Precautions When Using Radioactive Materials   For industrial sources:
1. Surround strong sources with a material such as lead or concrete.
2. Work behind shielding or at a distance from the radiation source.
3. Use remote handling techniques.
4. Monitor working area with, for example, a Geiger counter.
5. Monitor air content.
6. Wear protective clothing.
7. Limit time spent with source.

8. Have washing facilities available.
9. Wear a film badge – part of the film is covered by a cadmium shield which only γ rays can penetrate. The unshielded area will blacken more readily, being accessible to both γ rays and β particles. It is thus possible to distinguish between the dose of each of these radiations received by an individual. By including two films of different sensitivities one can check the dosage received weekly and over a longer period.
10. Maintain high standards of cleanliness.

Safety in Demonstrations
Sources used for demonstration purposes at G.C.S.E. level should:
1. *always* be handled with forceps;
2. *never* be pointed at an individual;
3. *always* be stored in a suitably labelled lead container when not in use.

Uses of Radioisotopes:

γ Rays
γ rays can kill bacteria in food. They can kill cancer cells in a patient. They can also sterilise medical instruments even after these have been sealed in a plastic container.

Carbon Dating
Carbon-14 has a half-life of 5600 years. Living things including plants take in and give out C-14 whilst alive. When dead, they no longer take in C-14; and by measuring the activity present in, for example, a sample of wood or linen, it is possible to estimate the age of it. Using a new method of carbon dating, laboratories in Arizona, Oxford and Zürich have recently shown that linen from the Turin Shroud dates from the period 1260-1390 and *not* from the time of Jesus Christ.

Thickness Gauge
The thickness of metal, paper and plastic sheets can be controlled automatically. If a G.M. tube is placed on one side of a moving sheet of material in line with a suitable radioisotope placed on the other side, then as the count rate increases the thickness decreases and vice versa. Appropriate instrumentation ensures the count rate is constant, i.e. the sheet thickness is constant.

Tracers
The progress of a radioisotope injected into a *system* (including the human body) can be followed using, for example, a G.M. tube. Tumours in a person take up more radioisotope than other parts of the body and so can be located.

Injection of a radioisotope into an oil or a gas pipeline enables leaks to be located.

11

3 Advanced Gas Cooled Reactor

Nuclear Reactor A nuclear reactor produces steam to rotate turbine blades on a shaft which also rotates to drive an electrical generator.

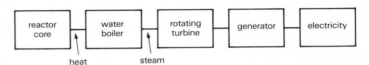

Boiler (Heat Exchanger)

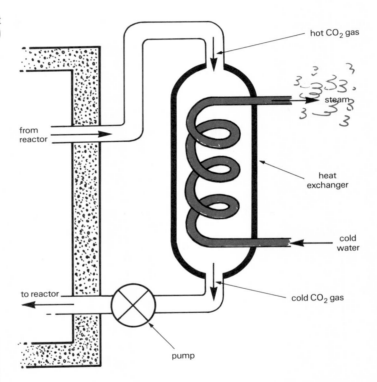

The pump drives cold CO_2 gas through the reactor core. It becomes hot and indirectly heats water in the heat exchanger, so converting it into steam.

Fuel Rods The fuel rods in a reactor are about 1 m long. Each contains 60-70 uranium oxide pellets having a length of approximately 1.5 cm and a diameter of 1 cm. In operational use the fuel rods have a surface temperature of roughly 850°C and can withstand temperatures > 1300°C.

Process of Fission Elements having $A > 208$ are capable of breaking into two approximately equal parts. This splitting is labelled fission. In 1 kg of natural uranium there are approximately 2500 spontaneous fissions every hour. Since all nuclei are in constant motion there is always a possibility that one will deform to a point where it will divide. This possibility is responsible for observed spontaneous fission in heavy nuclei.

Neutron Induced Fission Fission can be induced in uranium 235 or plutonium 239 by the capture of a neutron. Absorption of *slow* neutrons is more likely to occur than the absorption of fast neutrons.

Graphite Moderator If fission neutrons can be slowed down, we increase their chances of being absorbed and increase the probability of fission. Repeated collisions with some material ensure that a neutron gives up some of its energy at each collision. Such a material is called a moderator. A good moderator must not appreciably absorb the neutrons. Graphite is a good moderator. (Heavy water is used in some types of reactor.)

Common Reaction $^{235}_{92}U + {}^{1}_{0}n \rightarrow {}^{144}_{56}Ba + {}^{90}_{36}Kr + {}^{1}_{0}n + {}^{1}_{0}n + \text{energy}$

Ba and Kr are but two possibilities as daughter products.

$E = mc^2$ The mass of the fission fragments plus neutrons is less than the mass of U-235 plus neutron. The mass that is lost is converted into energy.

Energy released (E) = mass lost (m) $\times$ c^2, where c is the velocity of light. The fission of 0.5 kg of U-235 produces more energy than one million kg of coal.

Chain Reaction If neutrons from the fission of one nucleus split other nuclei, a chain reaction results. The end product is an enormous release of energy in a very short time interval.

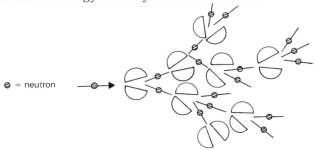

$\ominus$ = neutron

Some fission neutrons escape from the surface of the uranium before a chain reaction is set up.

Critical Mass The U-235 present has to be above a certain critical mass for a chain reaction to start.

13

Atomic Bomb   If two pieces of U-235 are brought together so that the composite is about the size of a cricket ball, the critical mass will be exceeded and the result will be an *uncontrolled chain reaction*. This is the principle behind the atomic bomb.

Reactor Schematic

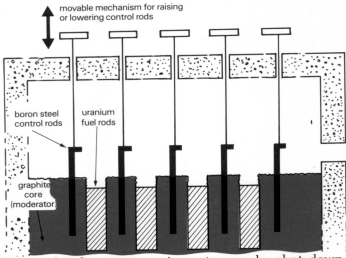

movable mechanism for raising or lowering control rods

boron steel control rods

uranium fuel rods

graphite core (moderator)

Boron Steel Control Rods   Boron absorbs neutrons. A reactor can be shut down by keeping the control rods in the lowered position. These rods are controlled by a mechanism which responds to changes in the number of neutrons present. In this way the heat energy generated by the reactor can be kept at a constant pre-determined level.

Safety Rods   In all reactors there is a safety rod (or rods) which operates independently of the others and can close down a reactor in the event of a control failure.

CO_2 Heat Exchange Fluid CO_2 gas is used to remove heat from the core because:
1. it is not very chemically reactive; and
2. it does not become radioactive by absorbing neutrons.
However, it does have a low *specific heat capacity* (see page 55) and therefore a large mass flow rate is required.

Automatic Shutdown   Automatic shutdown occurs to prevent boiler damage if the temperature at which the CO_2 leaves the core exceeds 700°C.

Enriched Uranium   Enriched uranium is natural uranium in which the proportion of the U-235 isotope has been considerably increased. Natural Uranium contains only 0.70% of U-235, the remainder being mainly U-238. Separating one isotope from a mixture of isotopes of the same element (enrichment) is very expensive, but economically feasible in the case of uranium.

Plutonium The fissile isotope $^{239}_{92}U$ is bombarded with neutrons.

$$^{238}_{92}U + ^{1}_{0}n \rightarrow ^{239}_{92}U$$

U-239 and Np-239 are both beta active.

$$^{239}_{92}U \rightarrow ^{239}_{93}Np + ^{0}_{-1}e$$

$$^{239}_{93}Np \rightarrow ^{239}_{94}Pu + ^{0}_{-1}e$$

Transuranic Elements Transuranic elements are elements heavier than uranium formed by neutron capture. They tend to have very long lives and emit α particles. Plutonium has a half-life of 25 000 years.

Breeder Reactors Breeder reactors are designed to produce plutonium as they run. Pu-239 has similar properties to U-235; when it absorbs a neutron it is capable of splitting with the production of energy and two or three neutrons.

Containment The reactor itself is contained in a steel lined concrete pressure vessel. The vessel cannot burst suddenly and minimises the escape of radioactivity. Protection against α, β, γ rays and neutrons is provided.

Nuclear Waste Radioactive sources tend to fall into two categories, intensely radioactive for a relatively short time period or more weakly radioactive for a longer time period. The isotopes strontium 90 ($T_{\frac{1}{2}}$ = 28 years) and caesium 137 ($T_{\frac{1}{2}}$ = 30 years) fall into the first category and so could pose a radiation threat to mankind.

High-level wastes are either:
1. liquid wastes arising from chemical reprocessing of the fuel (which entails separating waste products from uranium and plutonium); or
2. spent fuel elements.

Disposal of Waste
1. Initial storage for up to ten years in adequately cooled surface storehouses. (Radioactive decay generates heat.)
2. Final deep burial about 0.5 km down in stable geological formations.
3. Vitrification – converting the high-level liquid waste into a fairly stable glass, possibly clad with lead or titanium.

4 Forces and Motion

Force	A force is that which is capable of altering the state of rest or uniform motion of a body.
Units of Force	The unit of force is the newton (N) (see page 22).
Body	A body is a general term that covers whatever we want it to cover – a car, a truck, a bus, chairs, and so on.
Units of Mass	The unit of mass is the kilogram (kg).
Gravitational Field	A gravitational field is produced by any concentration of mass, e.g. a planet or star. The field will exert an attractive force on any other mass nearby, e.g. a spacecraft.
Strength of a Gravitational Field	The strength is defined as the gravitational force acting on a body in the field per kilogram of its mass.
Acceleration due to Gravity	Acceleration due to gravity is the downward acceleration (g) of a body attracted by the Earth's field (see page 21).
Weight of a Mass	Weight is the downward gravitational force (W) acting on the mass (m) during its descent. It still acts when the mass reaches the Earth's surface. From the definition of gravitational field strength:

$$g = \frac{W}{m} \quad \text{so,} \quad \boxed{W = m \times g}$$

Since W is a force, its unit is the newton. One newton is the weight of an average sized apple.

Strength of Earth's Gravitational Field	The strength of the Earth's gravitational field is about ten newtons for every kilogram ($\simeq$ 10 N/kg).

Over the Earth	
Mass (kg)	Weight (N)
1	10
2	20
5	50
100	1000

In fact, a more accurate approximation is 9.8 newtons per kg (N/kg).

Inertia	Suppose your Rolls-Royce and my Mini have both broken down on a stretch of level road. You would find it much more difficult to push your Rolls-Royce into a safe area than I would my Mini, and you would also find it more difficult to stop it after you had initiated movement. All matter has a built-in resistance to being moved if it is at rest or to having its motion changed if it is moving. This property of matter is called *inertia*, and the larger the mass of a body the greater is its inertia.

Mass of a Body   The mass of a body measures its inertia.

Mass and Weight   To convert masses on the Earth into weights, we multiply by ten (or, more correctly, 9.8). Since we would need to multiply the mass of *every* object in kilograms by ten to convert to newtons, it is simpler not to bother in everyday life.

However, in science:
1. we do not confine ourselves to the Earth; and
2. the gravitational field strength (denoted by the symbol g) *does* vary slightly over the surface of the Earth – for example, an object is pulled more by the Earth at sea-level than at the top of a high mountain, therefore its weight is greater at sea-level.

Surface Gravitational Field Strength

Planet	Surface gravitational field strength (N/kg)
Mercury	3.3
Venus	8.5
Earth	9.8
Jupiter	25.1

Average Speed

$$\text{Average speed} = \frac{\text{total distance travelled}}{\text{total time taken}}$$

Example Problem   Suppose a 360-kilometre road journey takes 5 hours. Our speed is continually changing depending on road conditions. What is our average speed?

Solution

$$\text{Average speed} = \frac{360 \text{ km}}{5 \text{ h}} = \frac{72 \text{ km}}{1 \text{ h}} = 72 \text{ km/h}$$

In the answer, the divider has gone and kilometres and hours have been brought together on one line.

Speed Conversions   Often it is convenient to quote speeds (and velocities) in metres per second as opposed to kilometres per hour.

$$72 \text{ km/h} = \frac{72 \text{ km}}{1 \text{ h}} = \frac{72\,000 \text{ m}}{60 \times 60 \text{ s}} = \frac{20 \text{ m}}{1 \text{ s}} = 20 \text{ m/s}$$

Average Velocity

$$\text{Average velocity} = \frac{\text{distance travelled in a given direction}}{\text{time taken}}$$

Displacement   Displacement is denoted by s and is the distance travelled in a given direction.

Tickertape Timer   A tickertape timer comprises a steel strip which vibrates 50 times per second and impresses dots via a carbon paper disc on paper tape pulled through it. Since the strip vibrates 50 times per second, adjacent dots are $\frac{1}{50}$ s apart in time.

Tape Chart for a Body Moving with Uniform Velocity

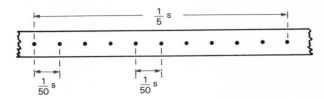

Equal distances are covered every $\frac{1}{50}$ s. The dot spacing is constant.

Acceleration

When the velocity of a body changes we say it accelerates. An acceleration is *positive* if the velocity increases and negative if it decreases. A *negative* acceleration is often called a deceleration or retardation.

A tickertape timer enables us to measure velocities and accelerations associated with, say, a truck on a friction compensated runway.

Friction Compensated Runway

A friction compensated runway is a runway tilted so that for *no accelerating force* the trolley neither accelerates nor decelerates.

Tape Chart for a Body Moving with Uniform Acceleration

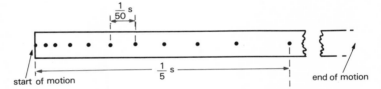

start of motion   end of motion

Imagine we have a long piece of tape to analyse. We normally cut the tape into strips (each strip representing $\frac{1}{5}$s).

Since average velocity equals distance travelled divided by time taken and since the time associated with each strip is a constant, it follows that the average velocity associated with each strip is directly proportional to the length of a strip. The 'steps' between adjacent strips give us a measure of the *change* in average velocity. If the steps are the same size the velocity has increased by the same amount every $\frac{1}{5}$s.

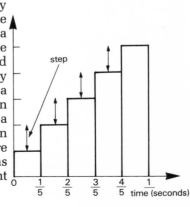

Definition of Acceleration

$$\text{Acceleration} = \frac{\text{change in velocity}}{\text{time taken}}$$

Units of Acceleration

The unit of acceleration is the $\frac{(\text{m/s})}{(\text{s})}$, i.e. the m/s^2.

Formula

$$a = \frac{v - u}{t}$$

where u = initial velocity,
v = final velocity, and
t = time period over which the change in velocity takes place.

Displacement-Time Graph for a Stationary Body

Let s = displacement covered in time t.

At time $t = t_1$ and $t = t_2$ (later), $s = s_1$.

Displacement-Time Graph for a Body Moving with a Steady Velocity

The displacement of the body is increasing by equal amounts in equal time intervals. This tells us that the velocity of the body is a *constant*.

Example

Consider two cars A and B cruising at around their top speed on a German autobahn. Car A is a production model and has a top speed of about 57 m/s*, whereas car B is capable of about 80 m/s*. Car B's figures are those of a Lister Jaguar XJS V-12.

*57 m/s = 129 mph
*80 m/s = 180 mph

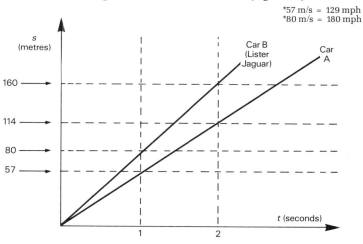

The steeper the slope the greater the velocity. The slope has dimensions of m/s associated with it. The slope (gradient) of the displacement-time graph yields the velocity of the body.

**Velocity-
Time Graph
for a Body
Moving with
Constant
Velocity**

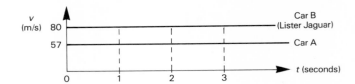

**Area beneath
a Velocity-
Time Graph**

Tabulation for Jaguar:

v (m/s)	80			
t (s)	1	2	3	4
Distance travelled (metres)	80	160	240	320

The area beneath the graph represents the distance travelled.

**Velocity-
Time Graph
for a Body
Moving with
Constant
Acceleration**

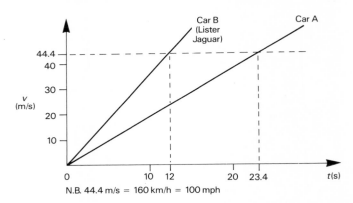

N.B. 44.4 m/s = 160 km/h = 100 mph

We are assuming that the velocities of the two cars increase by equal amounts in equal time intervals. The Jaguar's velocity is increasing by 3.7 m/s every second, and car A's velocity is increasing only by 1.9 m/s every second.

**Slope of a
Velocity-
Time Graph**

The greater the slope of a velocity-time graph, the greater the acceleration, i.e. the slope represents the acceleration of a body.

**Velocity-
Time Graph
Analysis**

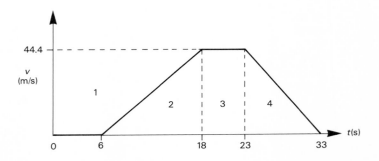

Consider the Jaguar. Let areas associated with regions 1-4 be labelled A_1, A_2, A_3 and A_4.

Region 1. Jaguar stationary for 6 seconds. $A_1 = 0$ m

Region 2. Jaguar moves from rest with a constant acceleration until $v = 44.4$ m/s.

$$a = \frac{v-u}{t} = \frac{(44.4 - 0)\ \text{m/s}}{12\ \text{s}} = 3.7\ \text{m/s}^2$$

$$A_2 = \frac{1}{2} \times 12\ \text{s} \times \frac{44.4\ \text{m}}{\text{s}} = 266.4\ \text{m}$$

Region 3. Jaguar moving at a constant velocity of 44.4 m/s.

$$A_3 = \frac{44.4\ \text{m}}{\text{s}} \times 5\ \text{s} = 222\ \text{m}$$

Region 4. Jaguar decelerates from 44.4 m/s to rest.

$$a = \frac{v-u}{t} = \frac{0 - 44.4}{10} = -4.44\ \text{m/s}^2$$

$$A_4 = \frac{1}{2} \times 10\ \text{s} \times \frac{44.4\ \text{m}}{\text{s}} = 222\ \text{m}$$

Total distance travelled $= A_1 + A_2 + A_3 + A_4 = 710.4$ m

Average speed $= \dfrac{\text{total distance travelled}}{\text{total time taken}} = \dfrac{710.4\ \text{m}}{33\ \text{s}} = 21.5$ m/s

Acceleration Due to Gravity (g) If we neglect air resistance all bodies falling under the force of gravity near the Earth's surface do so with uniform acceleration. Consider a ball *dropped* from the top of a building 45 m high. The ball will accelerate at a constant rate. Its velocity will increase by equal amounts in equal time intervals. In fact, the velocity will increase by 10 m/s every second (approximately). So after the first second its velocity will be 10 m/s. After the second second its velocity will be 20 m/s. After the third its velocity will be 30 m/s.

Equations of Uniformly Accelerated Motion Let us use the three equations of uniformly accelerated motion to find (a) the velocity of the ball just before impact with the ground, and (b) the time it takes before it hits the ground.

$$v^2 = u^2 + 2as$$
$$v = u + at$$
$$s = ut + \frac{1}{2}at^2$$

The height of the building is 45 m. In the equations s is displacement covered in time t. So, $s = 45$ m.

The ball is dropped from the building, so the starting velocity (initial velocity) is zero, i.e. $u = 0$ m/s.

Take the acceleration due to gravity to be 10 m/s^2.

(a)   Employ: $v^2 = u^2 + 2as$, but $u = 0$ m/s

$\therefore$ $v^2 = 2as$ (here $a = g = 10$ m/s^2)

$\therefore$ $v^2 = 2gs$

$\therefore$ $v^2 = 900$ m^2/s^2

$\therefore$ $v = \sqrt{v^2} = \sqrt{900} = 30$ m/s

(Taking the square root of *both* sides of the equation)

(b)   To find the time, we can use either:

$$v = u + at \qquad \text{or} \qquad s = ut + \frac{1}{2}at^2$$

$$30 = 0 + 10t \qquad\qquad 45 = 0 + \frac{1}{2} \times 10 \times t^2$$

$$\therefore t = 3\text{s} \qquad\qquad\qquad 90 = 10t^2$$

$$9 = t^2$$

$$\therefore t = 3\text{s}$$

Newton's 1st Law of Motion (NI)   Newton's First Law of Motion states that a body will stay at rest or continue moving with constant velocity in a straight line unless external forces make it behave differently.

The Acceleration a Body Experiences   The acceleration a body experiences is:

1. directly proportional to the net force F, acting (*for a fixed mass*); and
2. inversely proportional to the mass m (*for a fixed force*).

Mathematically:

$$a \propto F \quad (m \text{ constant}) \quad \text{and} \quad a \propto \frac{1}{m} \quad (F \text{ constant})$$

$$\therefore a \propto \frac{F}{m}$$

Thus: $\boxed{a = \dfrac{kF}{m}}$ where k is a constant of proportionality.

The Newton   The newton is defined in such a way that the value of the constant of proportionality k is 1. The newton is that force which will give a mass of 1 kg an acceleration of 1 m/s^2; so, $a = \dfrac{F}{m}$.

Newton's 2nd Law of Motion (NII)   Newton's Second Law of Motion is thus:

$$\boxed{F = m \times a}$$

Use of NII
Suppose that the force on an aircraft of mass 725 kg due to the engine is 15 000 N and suppose the size of the frictional drag forces operating is 9925 N.

frictional drag forces
9925 N

engine force
15 000 N

The net or *resultant* force is 5075 N.

Knowing $F = m \times a$: $\quad a = \dfrac{F}{m} = \dfrac{5075}{725} = 7 \text{ m/s}^2$

If the force due to the engine counteracted exactly the opposing frictional force, there would be no resultant or net force acting, so no acceleration would be produced. Therefore, the aircraft would travel at a constant velocity.

If the aircraft were capable of travel in outer space, then on turning the engines off, it would continue to move in a straight line (with whatever velocity it had achieved immediately prior to switching off the engines) for ever – provided there are no planets, asteroid belts or other heavenly bodies exerting a gravitational pull. Force is thus not required to keep a body moving with constant velocity so long as no opposing forces are operating.

Newton's 3rd Law of Motion (NIII)
Newton's Third Law of Motion states that if a body X exerts a force on body Y, then body Y exerts an equal and opposite force on body X.

Consider an object resting on the ground. The downward force W (the weight), called the action force, produces an equal and opposite upward force called the reaction R. An alternative way of expressing Newton's 3rd Law is to say, 'Action and reaction are equal and opposite.'

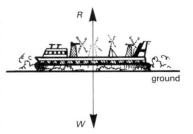

The weight of a hovercraft at rest on the shore is exactly balanced by the upward normal reaction of the ground. When the craft is in motion across the sea the same force balance exists but this time via the air-cushion sandwiched between the hovercraft and the sea. The air-cushion provided by the hovercraft considerably reduces friction between the craft and the sea, allowing it to travel faster than most ordinary boats.

5 Forces and Change of Shape

Tensile Force   A tensile force tends to stretch a material.

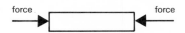

Compressive Force   A compressive force tends to squeeze or crush a material.

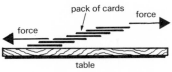

Shear Force   A shear force tends to slide one face of a material over an adjacent face.

The cards are in shear. A shear force can cause a material to slide, bend or twist.

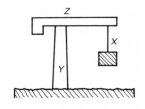

Crane   A crane can be reduced to three components:
1. a cable, X
2. a support, Y
3. a horizontal beam, Z.
X is in tension.
Y is in compression.
Z is in shear because it is acted upon by two equal and opposite forces, upwards from Y and downwards from X.

Beam   A beam is supported at each end.

The upper surface AB is in compression, and the lower surface CD is in tension.

Concrete   Concrete is strong in compression but weak in tension.

Concrete Beam   A concrete beam may break unless reinforced by including steel rods in the lower sections of the beam.

Cantilever   A cantilever is a beam supported at one end only. If the beam were concrete we would introduce steel reinforcing rods in the upper sections because they are in tension.

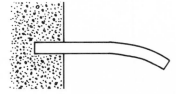

Equilibrium   If a particle or body has zero linear acceleration and no tendency to rotate, then the particle or body is said to be in equilibrium.

Atoms and Molecules Exert Forces on Each Other   Atoms and molecules in a material in equilibrium do not exert a force on each other, but if they are moved further apart than their equilibrium separation they attract. Similarly, if they are moved closer together (so that their electron shells begin to penetrate each other), they repel. When a material is in tension, the molecules of the material are further apart from each other than their usual equilibrium separation. Similarly, the molecules of a material in compression are closer to each other than their usual equilibrium separation.

Stress   Stress gives us a measure of the force with which the atoms or molecules at any point in a material are being pulled apart (tensile stress) or pushed together (compressive stress).

The stress in any direction at a given point in a material is:
1. directly proportional to the force acting in that direction; and
2. inversely proportional to the cross-sectional area over which the force acts.

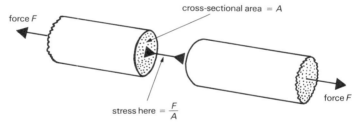

cross-sectional area $= A$

force F

stress here $= \dfrac{F}{A}$

force F

Units of Stress   The unit of stress is the newton per square metre (N/m^2).

Strength of a Material   The strength of a material is the stress required to break a piece of the material.

Strength Calculations   Strength calculations on a material enable an engineer to predict the strength of a structure.

Elastic Materials   Elastic materials return to their original dimensions (within certain load limits) when the deforming load is removed.

Examples   Examples of elastic materials include copper, mild steel and rubber.

Plastic Materials   Plastic materials show no tendency to return to their original dimensions when the deforming load is removed.

Examples   Examples of plastic materials include plasticine and lead.

Hooke's Law Hooke's Law states that provided some maximum load is not exceeded (the *limit of proportionality*), the extension of a material is directly proportional to the applied force.

Elastic Limit The elastic limit is the maximum load a body can experience and still retain its original dimensions when the deforming load is removed. The elastic limit often coincides with the limit of proportionality.

Testing Hooke's Law for a Vertical Spring

1. Hang the spring vertically alongside a vertical ruler.
2. Spring should have a pointer fixed to its lower end.
3. Increase the number of slotted masses on the hanger and record the corresponding extensions.
4. Ensure that on removal of each increase in mass the pointer returns to its original location.
5. Plot a graph of load (weight of masses) against extensions.

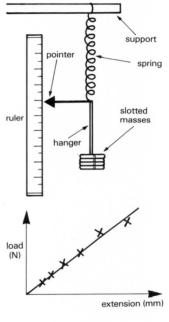

Force-Extension Graph for Rubber Rubber does not obey Hooke's law. It consists of long tangled chain molecules. It can undergo extensions ten times its natural length and still retain its original dimensions when the deforming load is removed. Stretching straightens out the chains. At X the chain molecules are fully straightened out.

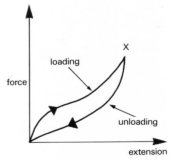

Ductile Material A ductile material can be permanently stretched by tensile forces.

Examples Examples of ductile materials include gold, copper and mild steel.

Force-Extension Graph for a Ductile Material

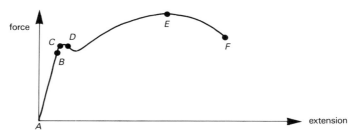

AB	Hooke's Law (linear) region
B	Limit of proportionality
C	Elastic limit
AC	Material behaves *elastically*.
D	Yield point. The material suffers a sudden extension for no load increase.
E	Maximum load applied to material
EF	Cross-sectional area of specimen decreases – necking may occur locally.
F	Fracture point. The stress at *F* is greater than at *E* because of the reduced cross-sectional area.
DF	Material behaves *plastically*.

Nylon Nylon is a polymer which is strongly resistant to tensile forces, does not corrode and is little damaged by impact. It also has a relatively high melting point, a low density and is fairly cheap. Hence, it finds uses as a climbing rope for example.

Brittle Material A brittle material breaks soon after the elastic limit has been reached.

Examples Examples of brittle materials include cast iron, brick, glass, ceramics and concrete. Brittle materials tend to be strong in compression. There is no noticeable yield point on a force-extension graph, and they suffer little reduction in cross-sectional area.

Force-Extension Graph for Brittle Material

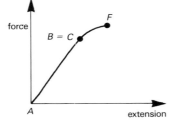

AB	Hooke's Law region
B = C	Limit of proportionality and elastic limit coincide.
F	Fracture point

6 Vectors and Vector Addition

Scalar Quantity   A scalar quantity has only size associated with it.

Scalar Addition   Scalar addition is straightforward. Thus 3 + 4 *always* equals 7.

Examples of Scalar Quantities   Scalar quantities include mass, length, volume, density, pressure, speed, temperature and energy.

Vector Quantity   A vector quantity has both size and direction associated with it.

Examples of Vector Quantities   Vector quantities include displacement, velocity, acceleration and force.

Vector Addition of Forces Acting in the Same Direction   Resultant force, R = 7N (to the right).

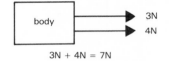

Vector Addition of Forces Acting in Opposite Directions   Resultant force, R = 1N (to the right).

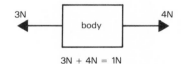

Vector Addition of Forces Acting at Right Angles   Resultant force, R = 5N (in the direction shown).

Here, the resultant is found by letting, say, 1N be represented by 1 cm. A rectangle is drawn and the length of the diagonal of the rectangle in cm gives the size of the resultant in newtons. It turns out to be 5. Alternatively, we could use Pythagoras's theorem:

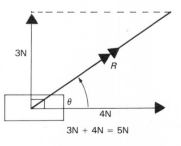

$$R^2 = 3^2 + 4^2 = 9 + 16 = 25, \quad \text{so } R = 5\text{N}.$$

Direction of the Resultant

The direction of the resultant with say the horizontal, angle θ, could be measured with a protractor.

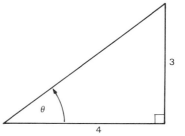

Alternatively, we know $\tan \theta = \dfrac{3}{4} = 0.75$. So $\theta = 36.87°$, i.e. the resultant force has a size of 5N and acts at 36.87° to the horizontal.

Resolving a Single Force into Two Forces at Right Angles to Each Other

Given:
$R = 5\text{N}$ and $\theta = 36.87°$
then $\cos \theta = \dfrac{X}{R}$,

so $\qquad X = R \cos \theta = 4\text{N}$

and $\sin \theta = \dfrac{Y}{R}$,

so $\qquad Y = R \sin \theta = 3\text{N}$

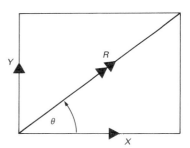

Parallelogram

A parallelogram is a four-sided figure with opposite sides parallel.

Parallelogram of Forces

The parallelogram law states that if two forces are represented in size and direction by the sides of a parallelogram, the resultant force is represented in size and direction by the diagonal of the parallelogram drawn from where the two forces act.

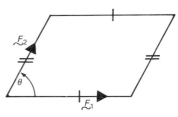

A scale diagram is usually drawn.

F_1 and F_2 are at θ to each other. The resultant R makes an angle ϕ with the line of action of F_1.

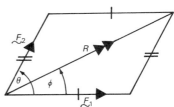

Vector Notation

Vector notation involves putting a squiggle or a bar above or below a quantity. For example a force F could be vectorially represented $\underset{\sim}{F}$ or $\tilde{F}$ or $\underline{F}$ or $\overline{F}$.

29

Typical Problem A sailing boat is steered at a steady speed due South. The force exerted on the boat by the wind has a size of 1500N in a direction 30° South of West. This force is balanced by:

1. a frictional force F_2 opposing the forward motion of the boat; and

2. a frictional force F_3 opposing the sideways motion of the boat.

Recall that for a body moving at a steady speed (i.e. not accelerating) there should be no net force acting (see page 22).

Find by calculation the sizes of the forces F_2 and F_3.

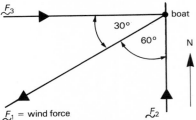

Solution The vertically resolved component of F_1, Y should counteract F_2.

$$\text{Cos } 60 = \frac{Y}{F_1}$$
$$\therefore Y = F_1 \cos 60$$
$$\therefore Y = 1500 \cos 60 = 1500 \times 0.5$$
$$= 750\text{N}$$

The horizontally resolved component of F_1, X, should counteract F_3.

$$\text{Cos } 30 = \frac{X}{F_1}$$
$$\therefore X = F_1 \cos 30$$
$$\therefore X = 1500 \cos 30 = 1500 \times 0.866$$
$$= 1299 \text{ N}$$

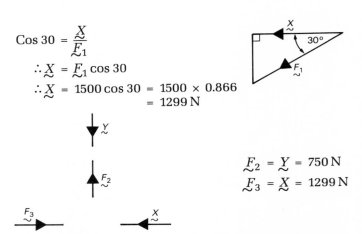

$$F_2 = Y = 750 \text{ N}$$
$$F_3 = X = 1299 \text{ N}$$

One could (less accurately) solve this problem with a scale drawing.

7 Moments, Centre of Gravity and Machines

Moment of a Force about a Point

The moment of a force about a point (torque) quantifies the turning effect of a force.

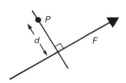

Formula

Moment of a force =	force × perpendicular distance
(about a point)	(from the line of action of the force to the point)

In the diagram, the moment of force F about point P is $F \times d$.

Units of Torque

The unit of torque is the newton-metre (Nm).

Riding a Bicycle

Riding a bicycle involves applying a force to a pedal.

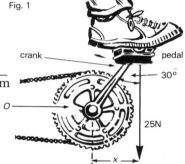

Fig. 1

Length of crank = 20 cm or 0.2 m. For a downward vertical force of 25 N, the moment about the bearing O is $25 \times$ Nm.

$$\sin 30 = \frac{x}{\text{length of crank}} = \frac{x}{0.2\,\text{m}}$$

$\therefore x = 0.1$ m

$\therefore$ moment about bearing O

$\quad = 25\text{N} \times 0.1$ m

$\quad = 2.5$ Nm

Turning the pedal to the correct position and applying the same force results in the maximum moment about the bearing.

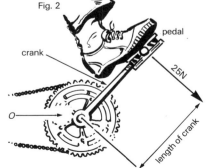

Fig. 2

Moment about bearing is 25 N × 0.2 m, i.e. 5 Nm

The greatest moment exerted by the bicycle rider is with the pedal as in fig. 2.

Principle of Moments
The principle of moments states that for a body in equilibrium, the sum of the clockwise moments equals the sum of the anticlockwise moments.

Parallel Forces Acting on a Body
1. The sum of the forces in one direction equals the sum of forces in the opposite direction.
2. The principle of moments applies.

Centre of Gravity
The centre of gravity (c.g.) is the point through which the total weight of an object appears to act.

To Find the Centre of Gravity of an Irregular Shaped Lamina
1. Let the card hang freely from a pin held in a retort stand.
2. Hang a plumbline from the pin.
3. Mark the position of the plumb-line with crosses on the card. Draw a line through the crosses. The c.g. of the card lies somewhere on this line.
4. Rehang the card with the pin through another hole.
5. Repeat 3.

thin sheet of cardboard

pin

plumb line (thread + weight)

The intersection of the two lines locates the c.g. We can check this result by rehanging the card through a third hole and repeating 3 once more.

Stability of an Object
The stability of an object depends upon:
1. the location of its centre of gravity; and
2. its base area.

Stable objects should have a low c.g. and a wide base area.

Racing Cars
Racing cars are built low. Their engines are usually mounted lengthways and nest in the middle of the rear of the car. They have a wide wheelbase and are shod with wide tyres. The risk of overturning when travelling around tortuous bends at high speeds is thus dramatically reduced.

Machine
A machine is a device for doing work.

Lever
A lever is a simple machine. A crowbar is the simplest form of lever.

Fulcrum
The fulcrum is the axis about which a rigid body is pivoted.

Effort (E), Load (L)
The effort E is the term used to describe a force applied at one point on the lever to overcome a force called the load L at some other point.

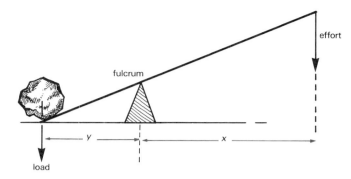

Equation of Moments about Fulcrum

The equation for load and effort about the *fulcrum* is:

$$\boxed{L \times y = E \times x}$$

where x = perpendicular distance of fulcrum to line of action of effort;

and y = perpendicular distance of fulcrum to line of action of load.

In practice $E \times x$ is *always* greater than $L \times y$ because of friction at the fulcrum and the weight of the lever.

Efficiency of a Machine

$$\boxed{\text{Efficiency of a machine} = \frac{\text{work done on the load}}{\text{work done by the effort}}}$$

(See Chapter 11)

Efficiency of lever above $= \dfrac{L \times y}{E \times x}$

The ratio is usually expressed as a percentage (multiply by 100).

Typical Levers

		Examples
Type 1.	Fulcrum lies between effort and load	crowbar, claw hammer, pliers
Type 2.	Load lies between effort and fulcrum	wheelbarrow, nutcrackers, car bonnet
Type 3.	Effort lies between load and fulcrum	fishing rod, tweezers, sugar tongs

Type 2   Type 2 levers are known as force multipliers because a small effort moves a large load.

Type 3   Type 3 levers are known as distance multipliers because the load moves further than the effort. The distance is magnified. (N.B. The load is smaller than the effort.)

Wheel and Axle	The wheel and axle is a continuous lever. Examples include the brace, the screwdriver, a car steering wheel, and the winch.

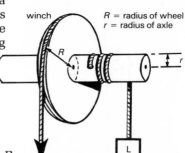

Circum-ference of a Circle	$C = 2 \times \pi \times$ radius Distance moved by effort $= 2\pi R$ Distance moved by load $= 2\pi r$

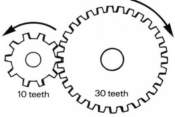

Equation of Moments about Axis of Rotation	The equation for load and effort about the *axis of rotation* is: $$\boxed{L \times r = E \times R}$$ $E \times R$ is always greater than $L \times r$ because of friction.

Gears	Gears can also be considered to be a continuous lever. The small wheel needs to move anticlockwise through three full turns for the large wheel to more through one full turn (clockwise).
Driver	The small wheel here is known as the *driver*. The large wheel is being *driven*. Reversing roles (large wheel driving small one) results in the small wheel rotating at a greater rate than the large one.

8 Solids, Liquids and Gases

Kinetic Theory of Matter
The kinetic theory of matter explains the existence and properties of the three states of matter – namely solids, liquids and gases. Electric forces acting between molecules (and ions) can be both attractive and repulsive. If two molecules are very close to each other they repel. At a particular distance the attractive and repulsive forces cancel. Beyond this distance attractive forces predominate. The size of the attractive force tails off quite sharply with increasing distance.

Solids
Molecules within a solid can vibrate only about a mean fixed position. The average distance between adjacent molecules is such that attractive and repulsive forces cancel. In metals the distance between the centre of an ion and its nearest neighbour is approximately equal to the diameter of one ion. The distance between adjacent ice molecules is approximately equal to two molecular diameters.

Solids have a regular repeating molecular or ionic pattern, i.e. they are crystalline. Solids have a definite shape and volume.

Properties of Solids
1. Close molecular packing.
2. Low compressibilities.
3. Densities – high compared to gases.
4. Rigid – they do not easily change their shape under the action of small forces.

Liquids
Liquid molecules have enough energy to move quickly over short distances and are never in the proximity of another molecule for a long enough period to be held in a fixed position. A liquid can flow and always takes the shape of its container.

Properties of Liquids
1. Comparatively close but disordered molecular packing.
2. Low compressibilities ($\sim$ same as solids).
3. Densities $\sim$ same as solids.
4. No rigidity.
5. Have viscosities about one hundred times higher than gases.

Viscosity of a Medium
A body moving through a medium has to keep pushing the medium aside to keep moving. If the force exerted on the body needs to be large to keep the body moving, the medium is said to have a high viscosity. Conversely, if only a small force is required, the medium is said to have a low viscosity.

Gases Gas molecules are usually a large distance apart compared with their diameter. Typically the average distance between adjacent gas molecules is about ten times the distance between ions or molecules in a solid. Gas molecules are capable of speeds of hundreds of metres per second.

Properties of Gases
1. Irregular spatial arrangement.
2. Highly compressible over wide ranges of volume.
3. Low densities (a small number of molecules per m^3).
4. No rigidity.
5. Low viscosities.

Units of Volume The units of volume are mm^3, cm^3, m^3, litres (l), millilitres (ml).

Volume of a Regular Solid

Cube of length l $\Rightarrow$ Volume = l^3

Rectangular block of length l, width w, depth d $\Rightarrow$

Volume = $l \times w \times d$

Sphere of radius r $\Rightarrow$ Volume = $\dfrac{4}{3}\pi r^3$

Cylinder of length l, radius r $\Rightarrow$ Volume = $\pi r^2 l$

Volume of a Small Irregular Shaped Solid Take a measuring cylinder. Fill to a pre-determined level with a liquid in which the solid will not dissolve. Immerse solid.

The difference between level 1 and level 2 gives the volume of the solid.

Volume of a Large Irregular Shaped Solid Use a displacement can (sometimes called a Eureka can). The volume of liquid collected in the measuring cylinder gives the volume of the solid.

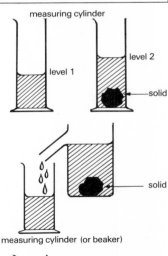

Volume of a Liquid Liquid volume is measured in litres or millilitres:
1 litre = 1000 cm^3,
so 1 ml = 1 cm^3.

Volume readings are always taken level with the flat part of the meniscus.

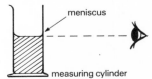

Volume of a Gas   A gas will occupy any container. The volume occupied by the gas is thus equal to the volume of the container. The volume of the container can be found by filling it with a liquid and pouring the liquid into a measuring cylinder.

Density   Different substances with the same volume have different masses. 1 m³ of water has a mass of 1000 kg. 1 m³ of mercury has a mass of 13 600 kg. Mercury is said to be 13.6 times as dense as water.

Formula   The Greek letter rho, ϱ, is used as the symbol for density.

$$\boxed{\text{Density} = \frac{\text{Mass}}{\text{Volume}}} \rightarrow \boxed{\varrho = \frac{m}{V}}$$

Sometimes d is used instead of ϱ.

Units   The unit of density is the kg/m³ or the g/cm³.

Density of a Solid   If you know the volume of a solid (see above) and its mass, its density can be found using the above formula.

Example Problem   The density of steel is 6500 kg/m³. Find the mass of a solid steel cube of side 0.05 m (5 cm).

Solution

$$\text{Taking } \varrho = \frac{m}{V}: \quad m = \varrho \times V$$

$$V = 0.05 \text{ m} \times 0.05 \text{ m} \times 0.05 \text{ m}$$

$$= 5 \times 10^{-2} \text{ m} \times 5 \times 10^{-2} \text{ m} \times 5 \times 10^{-2} \text{ m}$$

$$= 125 \times 10^{-6} \text{ m}^3$$

$$\therefore m = \frac{6500 \text{ kg}}{\text{m}^3} \times 125 \times 10^{-6} \text{ m}^3 = 6.5 \times 0.125 \text{ kg}$$

$$\therefore m = 0.8125 \text{ kg}$$

Density of a Liquid   For a given amount of liquid, the volume V is obtained and the mass m is measured. The density ϱ is given by the formula above.

Brownian Motion   Brownian motion is the erratic random motion suffered by microscopic particles due to continuous irregular bombardment by the molecules of the surrounding medium. Typical examples include pollen grains in water bombarded by water molecules and smoke particles in air bombarded by air molecules.

Diffusion   Molecules of all gases move freely and tend to distribute themselves equally within the limits of whatever is enclosing them. Have you ever been upstairs in a house and smelt bacon cooking downstairs? Wandering bacon molecules have made their way upstairs. The process of spreading is called diffusion. The distance between neighbouring air molecules in a house is so large there is plenty of room for bacon molecules and other odours to spread out. Diffusion can also take place in liquids.

General Gas Equation for a Fixed Mass of Gas

$$\frac{P_1 V_1}{T_1} = \text{a constant}$$

where P_1 = pressure exerted by the gas

V_1 = volume occupied by the gas

T_1 = temperature of gas in kelvin

If P_1 changes to P_2, V_1 to V_2 and T_1 to T_2, then:

$$\frac{P_1 V_1}{T_1} = \frac{P_2 V_2}{T_2}$$

Gas Laws   If the temperature of the gas is constant, $T_1 = T_2$, then:

$$P_1 V_1 = P_2 V_2 \quad \text{(Boyle's Law)}$$

If the volume occupied by the gas is a constant, $V_1 = V_2$, then:

$$\frac{P_1}{T_1} = \frac{P_2}{T_2} \quad \text{(Pressure Law)}$$

If the pressure exerted by the gas is constant, $P_1 = P_2$, then:

$$\frac{V_1}{T_1} = \frac{V_2}{T_2} \quad \text{(Charles's Law)}$$

9 Temperature

Temperature   The temperature of a body is a measure of its 'hotness'. It is a property of an object that determines the direction of heat flow when the object is brought into contact with other objects. Heat energy flows from regions of high to low temperature. Temperature is a measure of the kinetic energy of the particles (atoms, molecules or ions) that constitute matter.

Heat   Heat is energy possessed by a substance in the form of particle kinetic energy. The unit of heat energy is the joule (J).

Thermometer   A thermometer is a device for measuring the temperature of a body in degrees Celsius.

Liquid in Glass Thermometer   A liquid in a glass bulb expands along a very narrow uniform bore capillary tube when the bulb is heated.

Melting Point, Freezing Point   The temperature at which a pure solid substance melts is called its melting point (m.p.). The temperature at which a pure liquid substance freezes is called its freezing point (f.p.). They are the same thing.

Typical Liquids Used in Thermometers

Liquid	Freezing Point °C	Boiling Point °C
Mercury	– 39	357
Alcohol	– 112	78
Pentane	– 130	36
Toluene	– 95	110

Disadvantages   Liquid in glass thermometers have four disadvantages:
1. fragile;
2. unsuitable for surface temperature measurement;
3. unsuitable for monitoring rapidly changing temperatures;
4. unsuitable for *very* high and *very* low temperatures.

Advantages   Liquid in glass thermometers have four advantages:
1. easy to use;
2. direct reading;
3. portable;
4. inexpensive.

Ideal Liquids   Ideal liquids should:
1. be easily seen – alcohol, pentane and toluene are usually coloured to make them more visible;
2. not cling to the glass surface;
3. expand substantially for a given temperature increase;
4. have a low freezing point or a high boiling point or both.

Sensitive Thermometer
A sensitive liquid in glass thermometer must have:
1. a very narrow bore; and
2. a bulb of large volume.

Fixed Points
Two standard temperatures called *fixed points* are needed to establish a temperature scale.

To Calibrate a Mercury Thermometer
The ice and steam points are used. (Alcohol and pentane cannot be calibrated by steam.)

Ice Point
The lower fixed point on the Celsius scale is the temperature of *pure* melting ice under normal atmospheric pressure – taken to be 0°C. Impurities in the ice lower its melting-point.

Steam Point
The upper fixed point on the Celsius scale is the temperature of *steam* coming from water boiling at normal atmospheric pressure – taken to be 100°C. Impurities in water raise its boiling-point.

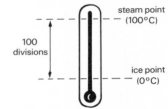

Clinical Thermometer
A clinical thermometer is used to measure body temperature.

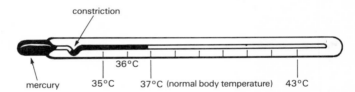

The scale extends to a few degrees on either side of 37°C. When the thermometer is placed under the tongue, the mercury expands and flows past the constriction. On removal, the thread of mercury to the right of the constriction cannot flow back and hence body temperature can be read. In order to use the thermometer again, we give it a sharp shake to bring the mercury back below the constriction.

Thermo-couple Thermometer
A galvanometer measures very small electric currents. The galvanometer deflection is dependent on the temperature of the heat source in fig. 1 or the difference in temperature between the hot junction and the cold junction in fig. 2. Thermocouples made from metals having high melting-points are used in industry to measure temperatures in excess of 1000°C. This type of thermometer is also useful for monitoring rapidly changing temperatures since there is only a small mass of metal to heat up.

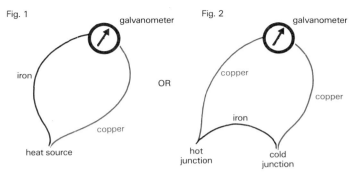

Heating a Solid
Heating a solid generally results in the array of molecules that make up the solid suffering:
1. an increased vibration rate; and
2. a larger amount of vibration about some mean position resulting in an overall expansion.

Contraction generally accompanies cooling.

Most metals are solid. Generally they melt under well-defined conditions of temperature and pressure to form liquids and boil at higher temperatures to form gases.

Heating a Liquid
Liquids also tend to expand with increasing temperature. However, water between 0°C and 4°C contracts and has a maximum density at 4°C. Beyond 4°C expansion continues.

A dramatic expansion occurs when water freezes and turns to ice. This can cause water pipes to burst in extremely cold weather.

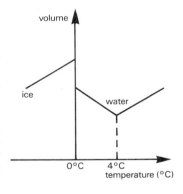

Heating a Gas
Gas molecules are randomly distributed throughout their volume. When they are heated, the pressure exerted by the molecules that make up a gas as well as its volume may change.

Bimetallic Strip
A bimetallic strip comprises equal lengths of two different metals firmly riveted or bonded together, e.g. iron and copper, or aluminium and copper. Copper expands more than iron and aluminium more than copper for a given heat energy input.

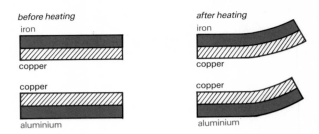

If the two metals in both instances had expanded equally no bending would have taken place.

Fire Alarm

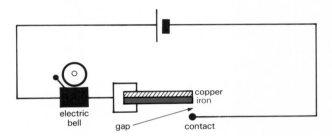

Heat from fire causes the bi-metal strip to bend, contact is made and the electric bell rings.

Thermostat A thermostat is a device used to regulate heat energy input where a constant temperature is to be maintained.

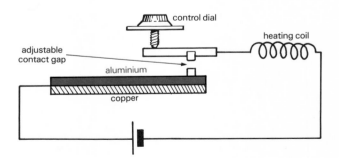

If the heater gets too hot the bi-metal bends away breaking contact, terminating current flow. As the bi-metal cools, contact is remade and current flow resumes. A reasonably constant temperature results. The electrical heating circuit of an electric iron works in this way.

Mercury Mercury is
1. a liquid; and
2. a good electrical conductor.

Liquid Thermostats Liquid thermostats often use mercury.

Electrically Heated Water Bath An electrically heated water bath often utilises a mercury switch thermostat to maintain a reasonably constant water temperature.

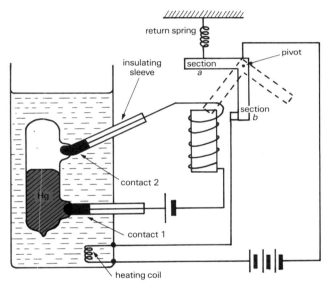

Operation
1. Initially, section *b* of pivoted (right-angled) armature *makes* heater circuit.
2. Water temperature increases.
3. Mercury expands.
4. Contact *2* is made.
5. Relay is energised.
6. Armature swings so that section *a* is attracted to the relay coil.
7. Heater circuit is *broken* – no current through heater circuit.
8. Water cools down.
9. Mercury contracts.
10. Contact *2* is broken.
11. Return spring pulls section *a* of armature back to original position.
12. Section *b* of armature *makes* heater circuit again. Process repeats.

Volume-Temperature Graph for a Fixed Mass of Gas

If we trap some air in a capillary tube with a sulphuric acid index and use a water bath to heat the air indirectly, we can raise the temperature of the trapped air. The pressure exerted by the air is approximately constant. The volume occupied by the air is directly proportional to l and so we can plot a graph of volume against temperature (see fig. 1).

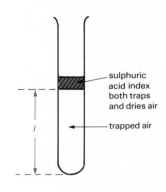

sulphuric acid index both traps and dries air

trapped air

Pressure-Temperature Graph for a Fixed Mass of Gas

A flask containing a fixed volume of air is heated indirectly in a water bath and is connected to a pressure gauge. The variation of pressure with temperature is noted, and a graph of pressure against temperature is plotted (see fig. 2).

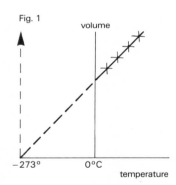

Fig. 1

volume

$-273°$ $0°C$

temperature

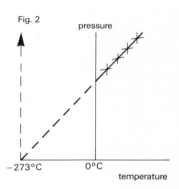

Fig. 2

pressure

$-273°C$ $0°C$

temperature

Producing the graphs backwards we find they cut the temperature axis at $-273°C$.

Absolute Zero

Absolute zero is the lowest temperature possible – the zero of the absolute or kelvin scale of temperature. It is equal to $-273°C$.

The Kelvin (K)

The kelvin is the unit on this temperature scale. A temperature difference of 1 K is the same size as a 1°C temperature difference.

Conversions

To convert from °C to K, *add* 273.
For instance:
$-20°C = 253$ K, $0°C = 273$ K, $20°C = 293$ K, $100°C = 373$ K
To convert from K to °C, *subtract* 273.

10 Pressure

Pressure Sometimes we have to consider not only the size of a force acting on a body but the area over which the force acts. Wearing snow-shoes or skis spreads a person's weight over a large area. The bigger the area over which a force acts, the less the pressure.

$$\text{Pressure} = \frac{\text{force}}{\text{area}} \quad \text{or} \quad P = \frac{F}{A}$$

Units of Pressure The unit of pressure is the N/m^2. 1 pascal (1 Pa) = $1\ N/m^2$.

Example Problem A rectangular block measuring 0.2 m × 0.3 m × 0.5 m has a mass of 20 kg. Calculate the minimum pressure exerted by the block on the ground.

Solution For the pressure to be a minimum, the area of contact should be a maximum. Taking the larger dimensions:
$$A = 0.3\ m \times 0.5\ m = 0.15\ m^2.$$
The force exerted by the block is equal to the weight of the block. Taking g to be 10 N/kg:
$$F = m \times g = 20\ kg \times 10\frac{N}{kg} = 200\ N,\ \text{and}$$
$$P = \frac{F}{A} = \frac{200\ N}{0.15\ m^2} = 1333.3\frac{N}{m^2} = 1333.3\ Pa$$

Pressure due to a Liquid
$$P = \text{depth of liquid} \times \text{density of liquid} \times g$$
$$P = h \times \varrho \times g \qquad (\text{Take } g \text{ to be 10 N/kg.})$$

At depth h: $\boxed{P = 10\,h\varrho}$

Note that the pressure due to a liquid is independent of cross-sectional area. The pressure exerted by a liquid at rest at a given depth acts equally in all directions.

Shape of a Dam The dam wall is thicker at the base. The arrows give a measure of the size of the thrust (force) at different levels within the water. (If we double the depth the pressure doubles.)

45

Example Problem	A tank 5 m long, 4 m wide and 3 m high is filled to the brim with petrol (density 800 kg/m^3). Calculate (a) the pressure exerted on the base, and (b) the thrust (force) on the base.

Solution   (a) $P = 10h\varrho = 10 \times 3 \times 800\,\text{Pa} = 24\,000\,\text{Pa} = 24\,\text{kPa}$

(b) $F = P \times A = \dfrac{24\,\text{kN}}{\text{m}^2} \times 20\,\text{m}^2 = 480\,\text{kN}$ (Since 1kPa = 1 kN/m^2)

Mass of the Atmosphere

The total mass of the atmosphere is estimated to be of the order of 5000 billion tonnes. The atmosphere is held in place by the Earth's gravitational field and begins around 800 km above the surface. It increases in density as we approach the Earth's surface and three quarters of the world's air is contained within the first 11 km.

Evidence for the Existence of Atmospheric Pressure

1. *Collapsing can.* If we remove air from inside a can, it collapses because the pressure inside is now less than outside.

to vacuum pump

2. *Magdeburg hemispheres.* In 1654 the German physicist Otto von Guericke, who was mayor of Magdeburg, evacuated the air from two large metal hemispheres to create a vacuum. Two teams of eight horses were unable to separate the hemispheres. Atmospheric pressure operating on the exterior of the hemispheres prevented them from moving apart until air was reintroduced.
3. *The wind* is a result of a bulk movement of moving air molecules which contribute to atmospheric pressure.

Atmospheric Pressure Decreases with Altitude

The density of the atmosphere is a maximum at sea-level (1.2 kg/m^3) and decreases with increasing altitude. If we assume an approximately constant gravitational field strength, then it follows that atmospheric pressure must decrease with altitude.

Pressurised Cabins

In aircraft cabins the air pressure is sufficiently increased to ensure the safety of the passengers. Cabin pressure is allowed to drop to around half of normal sea-level pressure when flying at around 11 000 metres.

Ear Popping

Ear popping is a consequence of a pressure difference across the ear-drum. Sweets offered to aircraft passengers promote swallowing, which facilitates pressure equalisation.

Spacesuits

Spacesuits are worn by astronauts in outer space and on the Moon (outside the pressurised space craft). They provide an appropriate 'atmosphere' for the astronaut. Without the suits, blood and body fluids would boil. Recall the boiling-point of a fluid (such as blood) decreases with decreasing pressure. In space few molecules of any compound bombard an astronaut (without a suit) and so the pressure exerted on him would tend towards zero.

Barometer A barometer is an instrument which measures atmospheric pressure.

Simple Mercury Barometer

A simple mercury* barometer is made by filling a glass tube (roughly 1 m long) with mercury, tapping out any air bubbles present and placing it upside-down in a mercury trough.

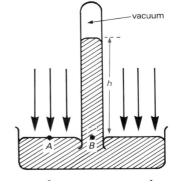

Atmospheric molecules bombard the trough surface exerting a pressure which supports a column of mercury in the tube.

Pressure at B = Pressure at A = Atmospheric pressure = $h\varrho g$.

*Mercury is used rather than water because mercury is extremely dense (13.6 times as dense as water). A water barometer would be over 10 m high!

Standard Atmosphere

A standard atmosphere corresponds with a height h of 0.76 metres or 76 cm or 760 mm. Atmospheric pressure is often quoted in millimetres of mercury (mm Hg). In a given location, the gravitational field strength and the density of mercury are taken to be constants and so the only variable is h. Atmospheric pressure at sea-level is about 760 mm Hg.

Bourdon Pressure Gauge

A bourdon pressure gauge works in a similar fashion to a rolled up party paper whistle which uncoils when you blow down it.

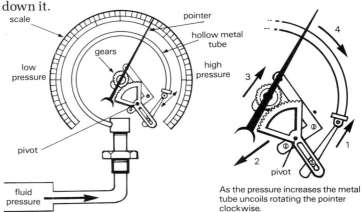

As the pressure increases the metal tube uncoils rotating the pointer clockwise.

47

Uses of Bourdon Gauge	A Bourdon gauge is used: 1. to monitor the pressure in boilers and gas cylinders; and 2. to monitor the oil pressure in motor vehicles. Note that Bourdon gauges have to be calibrated before use.

Aneroid Barometer

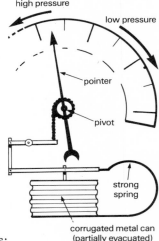

high pressure
low pressure
pointer
pivot
strong spring
corrugated metal can (partially evacuated)

An aneroid barometer comprises a partly evacuated flexible metal can with corrugated sides to increase its strength and allow it to expand or contract vertically. A strong spring prevents the can collapsing.

If the air pressure increases, the can caves in a little, resulting in the pointer rotating anticlockwise in the diagram. If the air pressure decreases, the spring pulls up the top of the can, causing the pointer to rotate clockwise.

Uses of Aneroid Barometer

The aneroid barometer is used as:
1. a wall barometer for houses (high pressure implies good weather and low pressure implies poor weather); and
2. an altimeter for aircraft – the higher the aircraft, the lower the pressure.

U-Tube Manometer

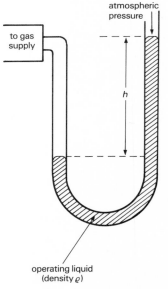

atmospheric pressure
to gas supply
h
operating liquid (density ϱ)

A U-tube manometer is a device for measuring differences in fluid pressure. For larger pressure differences the operating liquid would be mercury and for small pressure differences we might use water or oil. Suppose that one end of the U-tube is connected to a gas supply.

The operating liquid is pushed around the U-bend by the pressure difference. The pressure exerted by the gas is greater than atmospheric by h cm of operating liquid. To convert to Pa we need to quote h in metres and multiply by $10\,\varrho$ (i.e. $P = 10\,h\varrho$).

Head of Liquid

The height h is sometimes called the head of liquid.

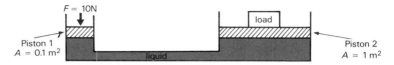

$$\text{Pressure of gas} = \text{atmospheric pressure} + h\varrho g.$$

Hydraulic Machines

When pressure is applied to a fluid in a given direction the fluid changes it into a pressure acting in all directions.

$F = 10\text{N}$

load

Piston 1
$A = 0.1 \text{ m}^2$

liquid

Piston 2
$A = 1 \text{ m}^2$

A is the cross-sectional area.

A downward force of 10 N acts on piston *1*.

The pressure transmitted through the liquid is given by:

$$P = \frac{F}{A} = \frac{10\text{N}}{0.1\text{m}^2} = 100 \text{ N/m}^2 = 100 \text{ Pa}$$

Thus a force of 10 N produces a force of 100 N.

N.B. The distance through which piston *2* moves is only $\frac{1}{10}$ of the distance that piston *1* moves through (conservation of energy).

Simple Hydraulic Car Braking System

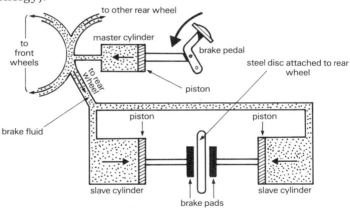

to other rear wheel

to front wheels

master cylinder

brake pedal

to rear wheel

steel disc attached to rear wheel

piston

brake fluid

piston

piston

slave cylinder

brake pads

slave cylinder

Operation

1. Depress brake pedal.
2. Master cylinder piston moves, forcing brake fluid through narrow pipes leading to the four wheels.
3. The slave cylinder pistons are pushed by the fluid.
4. Brake pads (normally held apart by a spring) are forced against the sides of a disc (which rotates with the wheel). The discs are not enclosed, and heat generated on braking is quickly dissipated into the atmosphere.

Air Bubbles

Air bubbles are compressible and if present in the system significantly reduce braking efficiency.

11 Work, Energy, Power and Efficiency

Work
Work suggests the application of effort to some purpose. In Physics, work is said to be done when a force moves a body through a certain distance in the *direction of the force*.

Formula

Work = force × distance (in the direction of the force)

$$W = F \times s$$

Units of Work
In the S.I. system the unit of force is the newton, and the unit of distance is the metre, so the units associated with work are the newton-metre or Nm.

The Joule
The joule is defined in such a way that when a force of 1 newton moves a body 1 m in the direction of the force, 1 joule of work is said to be done (1 J = 1 Nm).

Energy
Energy implies a fuel or even *power* in semi-scientific language; but in Physics, energy is a difficult concept. There are formulae for computing some numerical quantities but the quantities are abstract. However, we know that no work of any kind can be done without some energy being used.

Definition of Energy
Energy provides the capacity or ability to do work and is expended when work is being done.

Units of Energy
The unit of energy is the joule (J) – the same as the unit of work.

Power
Power in Physics has a very precise meaning. Consider two different machines, A and B. Each machine can perform the same amount of work; but suppose that machine A can do five jobs in the same time that machine B does one, i.e. machine A is doing its work five times as fast as machine B. We say it has five times the power.

Definition of Power
Power is a measure of the rate at which work is done or the rate at which energy is converted from one form to another, i.e. work done per second.

Formula

$$\text{Power} = \frac{\text{work done}}{\text{time taken}} = \frac{\text{energy used}}{\text{time taken}}$$

Units of Power
The unit of work (or energy) is the joule and the unit of time is the second, so the unit of power is the joule divided by the second.

The Watt (W)
The watt is defined to be a rate of working of 1 joule per second. We would normally quote power in watts.

Useful Multiples of the Watt

One kilowatt = 1000 W (10^3W)
One megawatt = 1 000 000 W (10^6W)
One gigawatt = 1 000 000 000 W (10^9W)

There are many different forms of energy (light, wave, nuclear, electrical, chemical, heat, sound, mechanical and so on) and we believe today that:
1 energy can be converted from one form to another; and
2 in such conversions the total amount of energy that we finish up with is the same as that we started with, i.e. we believe that energy can be neither created nor destroyed.

Principle of Conservation of Energy

The principle of the conservation of energy states that in an energy conversion, the total amount of energy present is a constant.

Efficiency

A perfect machine would be 100% efficient. In practice no machine is 100% efficient, since energy is always wasted overcoming friction between the moving parts of the machine. The input energy to a machine is *always* greater than the machine's output energy. If the input energy to a motor is 2000 J and the output energy is 1200 J, then the efficiency of the machine expressed as a fraction is:

$$\frac{1200\text{ J}}{2000\text{ J}} = \frac{120}{200} = \frac{12}{20} = \frac{6}{10} = 0.6$$

Note, efficiency has *no* units (joules on the numerator cancel with joules on the denominator). We would normally express efficiency as a percentage. To do this we multiply our result by 100 so the machine described above is 60% efficient.

Definition of Efficiency

$$\text{Efficiency} = \frac{\text{useful output energy}}{\text{input energy}} = \frac{\text{useful output power}}{\text{input power}}$$

Kinetic Energy

Kinetic energy (k.e.) is the energy a body has because of its motion. The faster a body moves the more k.e. it has.

Formula

$$\text{k.e.} = \frac{1}{2}mv^2$$

where m = mass of body (in kg)
v = velocity of body (in m/s)

Units of Kinetic Energy

The unit of kinetic energy is the joule (J).

Potential Energy

Potential energy (p.e.) is the energy *associated* with a body because of its position or condition.

Gravitational Potential Energy

A body above the Earth's surface is considered to have associated with it an amount of gravitational p.e. equal to the work done by the force used to raise it (against gravity).

51

To lift a body of mass m through a *vertical* height h requires a *force* equal and opposite to the weight of the body. If the local gravitational field strength is g, then the weight of the body is given by mg and the force required is equal to mg.

Recall our definition of *work*:

Work = force × distance (in the direction of the force)

Here, work done by force = force × vertical height
$$= mg \times h$$
$$= mgh$$

Formula   Therefore: $\boxed{\text{p.e. } = mgh}$

Units of Potential Energy   The unit of potential energy is also the joule.
N.B. We call the quantity gh the *potential* of the gravitational field at the height h.

Gravitational Potential Difference   Consider two locations in space above the earth (namely A and B) where the local gravitational field strength is g. Locations A and B are heights h_a and h_b above ground.
A mass m held at A has associated with it a potential energy mgh_a joules. The potential at A is gh_a joules/kg.

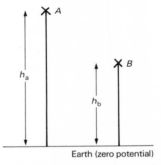

Earth (zero potential)

The potential differences between locations A and Earth, and B and Earth, are respectively:
$$V_a(= gh_a) \text{ and } V_b(= gh_b)$$
The potential difference between location A and B is $V_a - V_b$.

The gravitational potential difference between two points may be defined as the energy released per kilogram when an object falls from one point to the other.

Units of Potential Difference   The unit of gravitational potential difference is the joule per kilogram (J/kg).

2 Thermal Energy

Conduction of Heat
Heat conduction is the transfer of heat energy through matter due to a *temperature gradient* (see page 54). There is no movement of the matter as a whole.

Metals
Metals comprise relatively fixed ions in a sea of electrons. Heating one part of a metal results in a localised electron kinetic energy increase. These energetic electrons transfer some of their energy to atoms in cooler parts by collisions raising the temperature of these parts. Metals are the best conductors of heat.

Non-Metals
Non-metals contain no free electrons. The atoms at the hot part of a non-metal vibrate vigorously, transferring energy by collisions to cooler neighbouring atoms. However, this is a relatively inefficient process and non-metals tend to be poor conductors.

Fluids
In fluids (liquids and gases), high energy molecules collide with an energy transfer to 'cooler' molecules. Gases are much poorer conductors than liquids.

Convection
Convection is the process by which heat energy flows from one part of a fluid to another by the actual movement of the fluid. This movement is due to density differences.

Air
Air is a very poor conductor. Houses may be built with double-glazed windows (two sheets of glass separated by an air gap) and cavity walls (two walls separated by an air gap). Air is a poor conductor but a good convector, so plastic foam (containing air bubbles) is sometimes injected into the cavity. Loft insulation (fibreglass) contains trapped air and minimises heat energy loss through the house roof.

Radiation
Radiation is the way in which energy in the form of electromagnetic waves (mostly infra-red) flows from one place to another at the speed of light. A very hot object (e.g. a star) emits infra-red and ultraviolet light.

When radiation strikes an object:
1. some energy is reflected;
2. some energy passes through; and
3. some energy is absorbed.
The absorbed energy raises the temperature of the object.

Rate of Conduction of Heat Energy
The rate of conduction of heat energy through a material depends on:
1. the nature of the material – copper is a better conductor than aluminium, which in turn is better than steel;

2. its area A – the bigger the area, the greater the rate of heat energy conducted; and

3. the *temperature gradient* – this is the ratio of the temperature difference across the material divided by the thickness of the material. The bigger the temperature gradient, the greater the rate at which heat energy is conducted. If we characterise the nature of the material by k and the temperature gradient by G we can write:

Heat energy conduction rate $= kAG$

Units of Conduction Rate

The unit of heat energy conduction rate is the joule/second or the watt, and k is known as the thermal conductivity of the material.

Radiation Detection

When heat energy falls on the junction of two different metals (e.g. bismuth and antimony) connected to the terminals of a galvanometer, we note a deflection of the galvanometer needle. Heat energy has been converted to electrical energy. The size of the deflection gives us a measure of the heat energy received. If we join many junctions together in series we magnify the effect. A cone with a highly reflecting surface is fitted over the end. It is called a thermopile.

Thermopile

Leslie's Cube

A hollow metal cube has four sides, each having a different finish and can be filled with hot water. The radiation from each side can be monitored with the thermopile.

A dull matt surface is a good radiator, especially if black, whereas a highly polished silvery surface is a poor radiator (e.g. a kettle or teapot).

Good Radiators

Good radiators are good absorbers.

Vacuum Flask

A vacuum flask keeps hot liquids hot or cold liquids cold. It consists of a double-walled glass vessel with a vacuum between the walls.

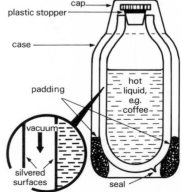

Radiation loss is reduced by silvering the inner (vacuum) faces of the walls. Any radiation in the vacuum gap is reflected back across the vacuum. The vacuum gap and the plastic stopper minimise heat energy losses due to convection. The materials that make up the flask are poor thermal conductors – glass, vacuum, plastic.

54

Greenhouse

Glass transmits short wavelength infra-red radiation. This is emitted by the sun and is absorbed by plants and soil inside a greenhouse which in turn emit infra-red but of longer wavelength. (Only very hot bodies are capable of emitting short wavelength infra-red.) The longer wavelength infra-red cannot penetrate the glass and the temperature inside increases.

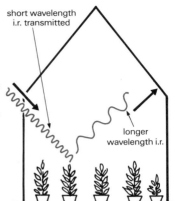

short wavelength i.r. transmitted

longer wavelength i.r.

Specific Heat Capacity (c)

The specific heat capacity of a substance is the amount of heat energy in joules required to produce a 1°C or 1 K temperature increase in 1 kg of the substance.

Units of S.H.C.

The unit of specific heat capacity is the J/(kg°C) or the J/(kgK). The s.h.c. of water is 4200 J/(kg°C). The s.h.c. of mercury is 140 J/(kg°C). This means that we need to supply thirty times more heat energy to raise the temperature of 1 kg of water than we would for mercury.

Formula

Energy required = mass × s.h.c. × temperature change

$$Q = m \times c \times \Delta\theta$$

The Greek symbol Δ denotes 'change'.

Example Problem

How much heat energy is needed to raise the temperature of 0.2 kg of water from 15°C to 20°C?

Solution

Given: $\Delta\theta$ = 5°C; m = 0.2 kg; and s.h.c. of water = 4200 J/(kg°C)

$$Q = 0.2 \text{ kg} \times \frac{4200 \text{ J}}{\text{kg} \times \text{°C}} \times 5\text{°C} = 4200 \text{ J}$$

Note how the units drop out to leave J. However, the kilojoule (kJ) is often used in the unit of s.h.c. and for Q itself; hence Q = 4.2 kJ. Note the kJ *is not* the S.I. unit of energy, whereas the kg *is* the S.I. unit of mass.

S.H.C. of Sea-Water

The s.h.c. of sea-water is approximately five times bigger than the s.h.c. of land. This means that it takes a relatively long time for the sea to heat up but a relatively long time also for it to cool down. This explains why islands do not suffer dramatic seasonal temperature changes whereas large land masses do.

Car Engine Cooling System

A car engine cooling system often uses water because of its high s.h.c. It is capable of taking in a large amount of heat energy from the engine before boiling takes place.

Central Heating System

A central heating system often uses water because the radiators connected to the boiler via pipes give out energy for a comparatively long time period because of water's high s.h.c.

Night Storage Heater

Night storage heaters contain concrete blocks (rather than the water of radiators) which are heated by elements at night when electricity is cheaper. Concrete is preferred to water since it releases the heat more slowly during the following day. The heat released is given by $Q = mc\Delta\theta$.

Determination of S.H.C. of a Metal Block by an Electrical Method

A 100-W electrical heating coil and a thermometer are placed in two appropriate cylindrical holes bored in a well-lagged metal block. In 3 minutes we observe a temperature rise of 40°C.

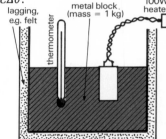

Solution

Heat energy supplied $= \dfrac{100\,\text{J}}{\text{s}} \times 3 \times 60\,\text{s} = 18\,000\,\text{J}$

So, for the formula $Q = m \times c \times \Delta\theta$, we know:

$Q = 18\,000\,\text{J}; \Delta\theta = 40°\text{C}; m = 1\,\text{kg}$.

To find s.h.c. (or c), rearrange:

$$c = \frac{Q}{m \times \Delta\theta}$$

$\therefore$ s.h.c. $= \dfrac{18\,000\,\text{J}}{1\,\text{kg} \times 40°\text{C}} = 450\,\text{J/kg°C}$

This is a little higher than it should be since we have not allowed for heat energy losses to the surroundings.

Specific Latent Heat of Fusion (l_f)

Sometimes when we supply heat energy to a substance we do not observe a temperature rise. Both ice and water can exist at 0°C. To convert 1 kg of ice at 0°C into 1 kg of water at 0°C we need to supply energy to break down the molecular bonds that characterise ice (the molecules are arranged in a regular ring structure). This energy is known as the specific latent heat of fusion (l_f). To convert m kg of water into m kg of ice we need to supply $Q = ml_f$ joules.

Units of l_f

The unit of latent heat of fusion is the J/kg (or kJ/kg or MJ/kg).

Water

Water has a specific latent heat of fusion of 334 000 J/kg or 334 kJ/kg. It also follows that if we want to convert 1 kg of water into 1 kg of ice we would need to remove 334 kJ of energy by cooling.

Specific Latent Heat of Vaporisation (l_v) The specific latent heat of vaporisation is the amount of heat energy needed to convert 1 kg of liquid into 1 kg of vapour without a change of temperature. Both water and steam can exist at 100°C. To convert 1 kg of water into 1 kg of steam at 100°C we need to supply 2 260 000 J or 2.26 MJ.

1 kg of steam has a much higher heat energy content than 1 kg of water. This is why a scald resulting from steam causes much more damage to skin tissue than one from boiling water.

Units of l_v The unit of latent heat of vaporisation is the J/kg (or kJ/kg or MJ/kg).

Cooling Curve of Naphthalene (a Pure Substance) Naphthalene gives off a toxic vapour and hence the experiment should be carried out in a fume cupboard.

1. Half-fill a test tube with naphthalene.
2. Place tube in beaker of water.
3. Heat water until all the naphthalene has melted.
4. Remove test-tube – hold in clamp.
5. Record temperature every half minute.
6. Plot a temperature-time graph.

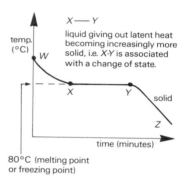

X — Y

liquid giving out latent heat becoming increasingly more solid, i.e. *X-Y* is associated with a change of state.

80°C (melting point or freezing point)

Naphthalene starts to solidify at 80°C. At *Y* on the graph naphthalene is completely solid and its temperature starts to fall again.

Cooling Curve of Paraffin Wax (an Impure Substance) Paraffin wax is a mixture of several waxes which freeze out from the liquid at slightly different temperatures resulting in a graph without a definite plateau region.

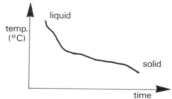

Effect of Pressure on Melting Point The melting-point or freezing-point of ice is *lowered* (very slightly) if pressure is applied.

Effect of Impurities on Melting-Point The melting-point (m.p.) of ice is *lowered* quite dramatically by adding salt. Adding antifreeze to a car water-cooling system reduces the risk of water converting to ice (with an accompanying dramatic increase in volume), and cracking the engine block.

Effect of Pressure on Boiling-Point Water boils at 100°C if atmospheric pressure is 0.76 m Hg. *A decrease in atmospheric pressure results in a decrease in boiling-point* (b.p.). The pressure of the steam above the water in a pressure cooker can be as high as 1.5 m Hg resulting in water boiling at 120°C. (This ensures food in the cooker is cooked more rapidly.) *An increase in atmospheric pressure results in an increase in boiling-point.*

Effect of Impurities on Boiling Point Sea-water has a higher boiling-point than pure water. Water containing antifreeze has a b.p. >100°C. *Impurities raise the boiling point.*

Evaporation Evaporation is a process which results in a liquid changing to a vapour. Evaporation can occur at temperatures well below the boiling-point of a liquid. Molecules within a liquid are attracted to neighbouring molecules, but because their energies are different the more energetic escape from the liquid surface, resulting in a decrease in temperature of what is left. Evaporation explains how snow and rain puddles can disappear even on a cold day.

Differences between Evaporation and Boiling 1. Evaporation is a surface effect. Boiling occurs within the bulk of a liquid resulting in bubbles.
2. Evaporation takes place at any temperature whereas boiling takes place at and above a definite temperature.

Factors that Increase the Evaporation Rate 1. Increased temperature.
2. Increased surface area.
3. Air blown across the surface.

Refrigerator

The *electric pump* drives freon vapour into the high pressure pipe where it condenses to liquid and gives out latent heat.

Cooling fins are usually painted black to radiate as much heat energy as possible into the surroundings.

The *constriction* turns the liquid into a spray (i.e. increases its surface area).

The *low pressure pipe* contains freon liquid. It takes in heat energy from the food inside the refrigerator and becomes a vapour.

13 Heat Engines

Heat Engines   Heat engines convert heat energy into mechanical work.

Car Engine   The car engine (internal combustion engine) is a type of heat engine. Petrol and air are mixed in a cylinder and compressed by a piston which slides freely in the cylinder. The mixture is ignited by a spark, burns, and expands forcing the piston outwards. A rod connecting the piston to a crankshaft converts the piston's vertical movement into a rotary one. The crankshaft rotation is transmitted to the wheels.

Compression Ratio of a Car

$$\text{Compression ratio} = \frac{\text{volume of gas in cylinder } \textit{before} \text{ compression}}{\text{volume of gas in cylinder } \textit{after} \text{ compression}}$$

The average family car has a compression ratio of about 9:1. The Jaguar XJ220 has a compression ratio of 10:1. The bigger the compression ratio, the bigger the power output.

Engine Variations   Engine variations include four cylinders in line, six cylinders in line (a straight six), and engines arranged in such a way that the cylinders make up a letter V: V-6s and V-8s are common. The Jaguar XJ220 has 12 cylinders arranged in a 60-degree V. The more cylinders involved, the more even the turning effort (torque). Vibrations are minimised and the ride is smoother.

4-Cylinder Engine   In a 4-cylinder engine the firing order is 1, 2, 4, 3 or 1, 3, 4, 2 (rather than 1, 2, 3, 4) in order to minimise stress and vibration encountered at engine and crankshaft mountings. Since all cylinders work in the same way we need consider only the operation of a single cylinder.

Single Cylinder 4-Stroke Petrol Engine Cycle:

Induction Stroke   Induction:
1. inlet valve open,
2. exhaust valve closed,
3. piston descends,
4. petrol-air mixture enters cylinder by atmospheric pressure.

The crankshaft continues to turn, forcing the piston up to compress the mixture.

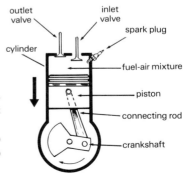

outlet valve

inlet valve

spark plug

cylinder

fuel-air mixture

piston

connecting rod

crankshaft

Compression Stroke

Compression:
1. inlet and outlet valves closed,
2. piston ascends,
3. sparking-plug ignites just before top of stroke.

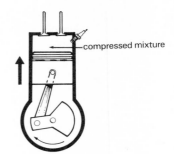

compressed mixture

Expansion or Power Stroke

The mixture burns and a rapid rise in pressure follows resulting in an expansion.
Expansion:
1. inlet and outlet valves closed,
2. piston descends,
3. crankshaft rotates.
This stroke is known as the expansion or power stroke.

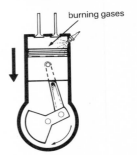

burning gases

Exhaust Stroke

Towards the end of the power stroke the exhaust valve opens. The crankshaft continues to turn and the piston forces the burnt gases into the exhaust system. This stroke is known as the exhaust stroke.

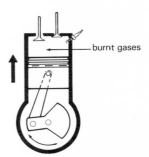

burnt gases

Starter Motor

A starter motor provides the initial work required for the first induction and compression strokes. Once the engine has fired, it will continue to work under its own power.

Crankshaft

The crankshaft makes two revolutions during the 4-stroke cycle.

2-Stroke Engine

A 2-stroke engine involves the petrol-air mixture being burnt on every downward stroke of the piston. The 2-stroke cycle is simpler than the 4-stroke but less efficient.

Summary

In a 4-stroke petrol engine cycle, mechanical work is extracted from a high-temperature gas (petrol-air mixture) in a cylinder. The gas is then discharged through the exhaust system at a lower temperature.

14 Energy Sources

Non-Renewable or Finite Energy Sources

Non-renewable or finite energy sources are the fossil fuels (namely, coal, oil and natural gas) and nuclear fuels such as uranium. These deposits are essentially fixed in quantity because they take millions of years to replenish naturally.

Renewable or Infinite Energy Sources

Renewable energy sources may arise from the sun directly (wind, wave, solar, tidal) and indirectly (biomass, geo-thermal), or be man-made (hydroelectric).

Nuclear Fusion

Nuclear fusion occurs when the nuclei of light elements merge forming more massive nuclei with an accompanying substantial energy release. Deuterons (nuclei of heavy hydrogen $_1^2H$) fuse readily into helium nuclei at temperatures of millions of degrees kelvin (temperatures existing in the Sun's interior). Thermonuclear fusion is the primary mechanism responsible for the Sun's radiant energy output and is also the basis for the hydrogen bomb.

Research into providing a controlled thermonuclear environment could eventually lead to a cheap power source.

Coal

Coal occurs mainly in large underground deposits. It consists of carbon and various carbon compounds. It was formed by the decomposition and compression of vegetable matter over many millions of years. On burning coal, stored energy, which came originally from sunlight, is released.

Oil

Early plants received sunlight energy and converted it into starch and cellulose. Marine organisms ate the plants and, when they died, their unused chemical energy remained. Over millions of years their rotting bodies yielded mineral oil.

Natural Gas

Natural gas is another source of chemical energy, formed from the plant and animal life of millions of years ago. It consists of about 95% methane. It can be piped and is widely used in industry and in the home for heating and cooking.

The Energy Crisis

Oil and natural gas reserves have a predicted lifetime of under fifty years. Coal will last perhaps a few hundred years. Nuclear power stations have a very short lifetime (under fifty years) and building new ones is very expensive. Research into alternative energy sources has thus begun.

Biomass

Biomass is the name for organic (and other) material from which biofuels can be obtained. For example, alcohol is derived from sugar cane. In Brazil, many cars run on alcohol instead of petrol.

Solid Biofuels Solid biofuels include wood and straw. They are burnt for heating.

Liquid Biofuels Liquid biofuels include methane gas and alcohol. They burn more efficiently at low temperatures.

Photo-synthesis Photosynthesis is the process whereby plants take in CO_2 and water from their surroundings in the presence of sunlight, and convert them into oxygen and carbohydrates (starches and sugars).

Efficient Fuel Crops Efficient fuel crops include sugar-cane and sugar-beet which convert about 6% of the solar energy that falls on them into stored carbohydrate energy, unlike most plants in temperate climates which convert less than 1%.

Eating Carbo-hydrates Eating carbohydrates synthesised by plants in the form of a plant or the flesh of a plant-eating animal results in a chemical reaction with oxygen which provides us with the food energy we need for all our body and brain functions.

Energy Values of Fuels and Food

Fuel	MJ/kg		Foodstuff	MJ/kg
Coal	30		Fresh fruit	2
Natural Gas	56		Green vegetables	1.5
Petrol	50		Milk	3
Wood	15		Cheese	17
			Eggs	7
			Sugar	16
			Bread	10
			Chocolate	23
			Beef	6

'Average' Person The average person requires an energy input $\simeq$ 10MJ/day.

Wind Wind is a large-scale atmospheric convection effect. Cloudless regions, heated more by sunlight than cloudy regions, have lower density and thus lower pressure (since pressure is directly proportional to density). Air flows as wind from higher pressure cloudy regions to lower pressure cloudless regions.

Windmills These can convert wind energy into electrical energy.

Windmill Types
1. Horizontal axis machines are the most common.
2. Vertical axis machines respond to wind from any direction (see Darrieus type on page 63).

Windmill Power
If D is the windmill diameter, V is the wind speed and ϱ is the air density, then the power can be shown to be proportional to $D^2 V^3 \varrho$.

Darrieus Type Windmill
The Darrieus type windmill is a sophisticated vertical axis windmill (curved blade, egg whisk shaped).

rotates about this axis

massive base for stability

rotatable blade

Offshore Wind Turbines
Wind speed offshore is greater than it is over land. In water depths of 5 to 35 m, offshore wind turbines could produce enough electricity to supply all the needs of the U.K. However, investment capital, operation and maintenance is at present too expensive.

Problems with Wind Turbines
1. Large wind turbines may be environmentally unacceptable.
2. The alternative is an array, or wind farm, comprising several hundred smaller turbines.
3. The spacing and configuration of such an array has its own problems:
   (i) wind turbines operating downwind of others suffer an output reduction; and
   (ii) the airflow pattern over other machines can be altered as a result of turbulence.
4. Tens of thousands of small wind turbines would be needed to match the annual energy output of a major power station.

Geothermal Energy
Geothermal energy is energy obtained from hot rocks. U-238, U-235, Th-232 and K-40 are naturally occurring radioactive elements concentrated especially in crustal rocks. These elements undergo continuous spontaneous decay and are responsible for the Earth's internal heat.

Aquifer
An aquifer is a water-bearing stratum (e.g. sandstone or limestone).

Hot Aquifer
A hot aquifer is an aquifer in contact with hot rocks.

Geothermal Heat Source
A geothermal heat source is indicated by the presence of volcanoes, earthquake activity, natural geysers and hot springs.

Tapping Geothermal Energy
1. A hot aquifer may be tapped directly.
2. An explosion may be detonated in hot solid rock below an aquifer, shattering the rock. Water from the aquifer seeps deeper into the hot solid rock, producing steam at a higher

pressure. A second borehole feeds in fresh water to maintain aquifer pressure.

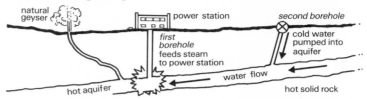

N.B. Temperature of the Earth's crust increases with depth.

Lardarello

Lardarello in Italy is the site of the world's first geothermal power-station, operational since 1904. The field produces superheated steam which is fed directly to turbines to produce electricity.

Indirect Space Heating

In Paris, hot saline water at depths ~ 2 km is extracted, passed through a heat exchanger (to eliminate corrosion problems) and reinjected into a second borehole. Hundreds of apartments are heated indirectly using this technique.

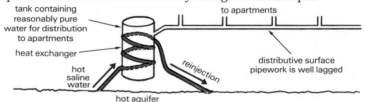

Problems

1. It is known from geological surveys in the U.K. that very few hot deep aquifers lie conveniently close to major cities.
2. It is expensive to transport over long distances the hot water given out.

Solar Energy

Solar energy is energy received directly from the Sun mainly in the form of light, infra-red and ultraviolet radiation. Solar energy has the advantage of being inexhaustible, non-polluting and free.

Solar Cell

A solar cell is a device for converting sunlight directly into electricity. A conversion efficiency of 10% is typical. A light meter uses solar cells, and so do communication satellites which power radio transmitters and receivers.

Solar Panel

A solar panel is a device for producing domestic hot water. In the northern hemisphere it is typically installed on the south-facing roof of a house.

Short wavelength infra-red from the sun penetrates the glass cover and most of it is absorbed by the blackened copper piping. The i.r. re-radiated is longer in wavelength (because of the low temperature) and cannot penetrate the glass.

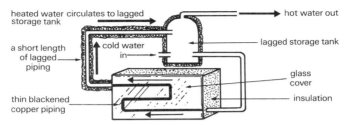

Thin blackened* copper piping contains the water to be heated. (Copper has a high thermal conductivity.) The piping is coiled in such a way that the area presented is a maximum. The rate at which heat energy is transferred depends directly on the surface area presented.

*Black surfaces are good absorbers.

Solar Furnace

A solar furnace is a device for concentrating the sun's rays on very small targets in order to produce high temperatures. A parabolic mirror focuses the rays on to a small target area in front of the mirror. In this way, temperatures in excess of 3000°C can be achieved. A boiler placed at the focus produces steam which can drive a turbine. A generator coupled to the turbine can produce electricity.

Factors influencing the Amount of Solar Energy Received

The amount of solar energy received at a point on the Earth's surface is affected by: the altitude; the time of day; the season; the latitude; and the degree of cloud cover.

Solar Power Station

A solar power station could comprise a large satellite (operating in continuous sunlight) in a geostationary orbit*, carrying thousands of solar cells to collect solar energy and convert it to electricity. This, in turn, would be beamed to a receiving station on the Earth in the form of microwaves.

*Orbiting at such an altitude that it remains stationary over a given point on the earth.

Tidal Power

Tidal power is a result of:
1. a gravitational attractive force between the Moon and the Earth (the Sun and the planets also play a lesser role); and
2. a rotating Earth – different parts of the Earth pass in and out of a bulge at different times – hence tides.

Oceans here are more strongly attracted (than average) to the Moon

Moon   Earth

Oceans here are less strongly attracted (than average) to the Moon

N.B. Take the centre of the Earth as under average pull.

65

A river estuary or inlet is dammed in such a way that high tide water is trapped. At low tide the water flows out. The potential energy of the water falling from a high to a low level is converted to kinetic energy by rotating a turbine, which in turn drives a generator, producing electrical energy.

Problems The power output depends on the tides (which vary on a daily basis) and is consequently intermittent. Economically justifiable tidal energy conversion requires:
1. a high tidal range;
2. a large number of estuaries or inlets which can be dammed; and
3. highly efficient turbo-generators that can operate at a low head of water.

Wave Energy Wave energy is a result of winds blowing across the sea causing waves. Floats moving up and down with the waves could convert this movement into electricity. However, tens of kilometres of floats would be needed to match the power output of a major power station.

Hydroelectric Power Rain-water stored in dams is piped (a tunnel through a hill or a mountain is equivalent to a pipe) from a high level to a low level. The mechanism for conversion to electrical power is the same as that described for tidal power.

The power available is directly proportional to:
1. the head of water – the vertical height through which the water falls; and
2. the water flow rate.

Pumped Storage Because steam pressure takes time to build up in a furnace, the power output of a large thermal power-station (one using coal, oil or uranium) cannot be quickly altered. It therefore maintains a baseload, that is, it never completely shuts down. At night, when demand is less than the baseload, surplus electrical energy operates pumps which raise water at mountain power-stations from the low level to the high level reservoir. When demand rises in daytime, the water previously pumped up is fed down to power turbines which are coupled to generators. The baseload is supplemented. This is known as pumped storage.

15 Wave Properties

Wave Motion Wave motion is the propagation of a periodic disturbance carrying *energy*. A periodic oscillation about an average position takes place at any point along the path of a wave motion. Sound waves in air are a consequence of oscillating air molecules. Similarly, water waves are a consequence of oscillating water molecules.

Progressive Wave A progressive wave is one that travels through a medium and transfers energy from one location to another. In a material medium (i.e. a non-vacuum), the particles of the medium oscillate and by virtue of this oscillation transmit energy.

Transverse Wave Motion A transverse wave motion involves particles vibrating at right angles to the direction of wave propagation.

Examples include water waves and electromagnetic waves.

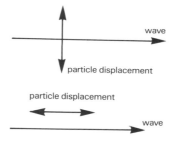

Longitudinal Wave Motion A longitudinal wave motion involves particles vibrating in the same direction as the wave.

A tuning-fork or a loudspeaker cone generates a sound wave in air. Air particles oscillate about some mean position as a wave passes, but the mean position of the air molecules does not move. Alternate layers of air at a pressure slightly higher than atmospheric pressure (compressions) and slightly lower (rarefactions) result.

Undisturbed Layers of Air (Before Passage of Sound Wave)

Situation After a Sound Wave Passes

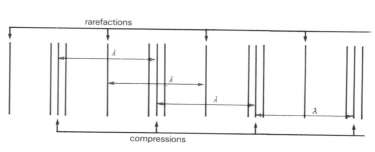

Slinky Spring   A slinky spring is capable of exhibiting both longitudinal and transverse modes of propagating energy.

Amplitude   The amplitude is the maximum displacement of a particle from the rest position. In a progressive wave, the particles of the medium oscillate with the same amplitude, but out of step with their neighbours.

Wave Profile Schematic for a Transverse Wave

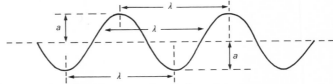

A water wave is one example of a transverse wave.
a = amplitude = height of a crest or depth of a trough above or below the average water level.

Wavelength   The wavelength is the distance between two successive crests or troughs or between two successive points on the wave which are in step with each other. Wavelength is usually denoted by the Greek letter λ (lambda).
N.B. for sound waves, λ is the distance between the centres of successive compressions or rarefactions.

Frequency   The frequency is the number of vibrations made per second by the wave source and hence also by the wave itself. The unit of frequency is the hertz (Hz). The unit was formerly cycles per second (c.p.s.). Frequency is usually denoted by f.

Velocity = $f \times \lambda$

$$\text{Velocity} = \text{frequency } f \times \text{wavelength } \lambda$$
$$\text{(m/s)} \quad \text{(in hertz)} \quad \text{(in metres)}$$

The velocity of propagation of a given type of wave depends upon the nature of the medium. Sound waves travel at around 330 m/s in air, 1500 m/s in water and 6000 m/s in steel. In a given medium the velocity is a constant, and it thus follows that if the frequency increases the wavelength decreases, and vice versa.

Reflection of Plane Wavefronts at a Plane Surface

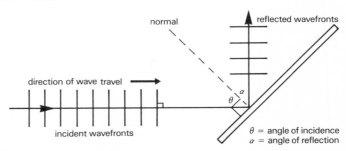

θ = angle of incidence
α = angle of reflection

Generate plane or straight waves in a ripple tank or a bath of water with a rectangular block of wood that is long compared to its width. Allow the waves to collide with a straight metal barrier.

We find that θ is equal to α.

Reflection of Circular Wavefronts at a Plane Surface

Generate circular pulses in a ripple tank, using a syringe. Observe what happens to the pulses when they impinge upon a straight metal barrier.

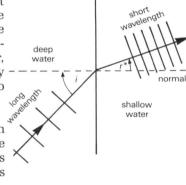

straight metal barrier

The reflected pulse appears to come from Y which is as far behind the barrier as X is in front.

Deep Water/ Shallow Water Interface

Generate plane waves in a ripple tank. The frequency at which the plane waves are being generated is fixed. Since the wavelength λ has decreased in the shallow water, it follows that the velocity of propagation has also decreased, since $v = f \times \lambda$.

The direction of propagation of the water waves in the shallow region is bent towards the normal. This 'bending' is termed refraction.

i = angle of incidence
r^* = angle of refraction

When the water waves meet the shallow region they are slowed down. So as the wave in the deep water travels the distance WX, the wave in the shallow region travels the shorter distance YZ.

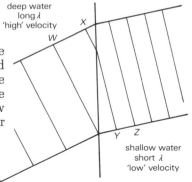

16 Mechanical Oscillations

Mass Spring System
The mass spring system consists of a loaded spring attached to a support.

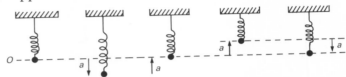

Displacing the load downwards through a distance *a* results in the load oscillating about *O*.

One Complete Oscillation
One complete oscillation involves the load moving through a distance 4*a* in a complete to and fro vibration between two points a distance 2*a* apart.

Amplitude of Oscillation
The amplitude of the oscillation is the maximum displacement attained by the load and is equal to *a*.

Time Period for One Oscillation (*T*)
The time period for one oscillation is the time taken to cover 4*a*. In practice one would need to time, say, 20 oscillations and divide by 20 in order to arrive at a realistic value for *T*. This is because the 'reaction time' involved in switching on and off a stopwatch can be of the same order of magnitude as T.

Frequency of Oscillation (*f*)
The frequency of oscillation is the reciprocal of the time period *T*. It is the number of oscillations made per second. *f* is measured in hertz (Hz). It can be shown that *f* is inversely proportional to the square root of the mass of the load.

Formula

$$f \propto \frac{1}{\sqrt{m}}$$

The natural frequency of vibration of the spring also depends on the nature of the spring – what is made of, and how thick it is.

Pendulum Bob
A pendulum bob pushed gently to one side of the vertical also oscillates with a natural frequency. Here, *f* depends on the length of the pendulum.

Barton's Pendulums

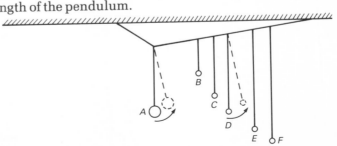

Set *A* oscillating. Pendulums *B-F* oscillate as a result. Pendulum *D* having the same length as *A*, and thus the same natural frequency, is set into large amplitude of vibration by *A*. We say that *D* has been set into *resonance* by *A*.

Resonance   Resonance occurs when a system is made to oscillate at its natural frequency as a consequence of oscillations received from another source of the same frequency.

A Child on a Swing   The child experiences increasingly bigger oscillations if the 'forcing frequency' of the parent is the same as the natural frequency of the child plus swing.

Domestic Spin Driers   Driers invariably pass through a speed equal to the natural frequency of vibration of the tub's elastic mounting causing it to vibrate violently for a few seconds.

An Unbalanced Car Wheel   The wheel eventually rotates at a speed equal to the natural frequency of vibration of the suspension system. The vehicle resonates and a sudden increase in noise is heard in the car.

A Diver   A diver gains substantial uplift by jumping repeatedly at the end of a diving-board. Eventually, the forcing frequency of the diver and the natural frequency of vibration of the board are equal, and resonance results.

Bridges   Bridges collapse if the frequency of one of the upward and downward forces resulting from incident wind matches one of its natural frequencies of vibration.

Soldiers   Soldiers crossing a suspension bridge should break step to minimise the possibility of setting the bridge into resonance.

Singers   Singers can shatter wine glasses if the frequency of the note is equal to the natural frequency of the glass.

Diatomic Molecules   Diatomic molecules such as HCl can be thought of in terms of a mass H connected by a tethered spring to Cl.

Molecules such as this can be made to resonate by subjecting them to infra-red radiation of a particular (known) frequency. The bigger the resonant frequency, the stiffer the molecular bond.

Minor Resonances   Minor resonances can occur in machines with rotating parts, if the (variable) machine frequency coincides with the natural frequency of one of its parts, or a simple multiple of this.

17 Sound Waves

Sound   Sound is a physiological sensation received by the ear. Vibrating bodies produce sound waves which are transmitted as a longitudinal pressure wave through a material medium. The ear detects sound waves and converts the pressure fluctuations into electrical impulses which are then decoded by the brain.

Sources of Sound   Typical examples include: the violin, the human voice, pneumatic drills, and church bells.

Sound Waves Require a Material Medium for their Propagation   This is another way of saying that sound cannot travel through a vacuum. This can easily be demonstrated.

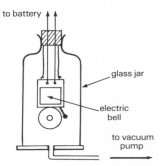

1. Switch on the bell.
2. Gradually remove air from the glass jar.
3. Although the striker continues to hit the gong, the sound slowly dies away.

Limits of Audibility   Humans are capable of hearing sounds with frequencies in the range 20 Hz – 20 000 Hz. The upper limit varies between individuals and generally declines with age. Some animals communicate by sound vibrations outside this frequency range either by ultrasonic waves above 20 000 Hz or by infrasonic ones below 20 Hz. Whales, dolphins, bats and many insects can hear well beyond the human upper frequency limit.

Echoes   Hard flat surfaces reflect sound waves well. An echo is the sound heard after reflection.

Echo-Sounding   Echo-sounding is used by ships to find the depth of the sea, i.e. to locate the sea-bed.

Example Problem   A ship transmits a sound wave, receiving an echo after 4 seconds. What is the depth of the water?

Solution   It takes 2 seconds for the sound wave to reach the sea-bed. Take the speed of sound in water to be 1500 m/s.

Using: $\boxed{\text{Speed} = \dfrac{\text{distance}}{\text{time}}}$

Rearrange: Distance = speed × time

$$= \frac{1500\ \text{m}}{\text{s}} \times 2\ \text{s} = 3000\ \text{metres}$$

Ultrasonic Echo Location   Bats emit ultrasonic pulses and navigate by listening to the resulting echoes. Blind bats navigate equally as well as those with sight. They also detect and intercept flying insects by the same means. Blind bats do not go hungry!

Oscilloscope   An oscilloscope (see Chapter 21) is a useful device for pictorially depicting transverse waves having the same frequency as the longitudinal sound waves associated with a sound source.

Loudness
1. Connect a microphone to the oscilloscope.
2. Whistle a soft note into the microphone.
3. Now whistle the same note louder.

Fig. 1

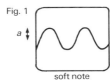
soft note

a and *a'* represent amplitudes. The *loudness* of a note depends on the amplitude of the wave.

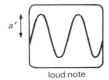
loud note

$a' > a$

Pitch
4. Sound a low-frequency tuning-fork.
5. Sound a high-frequency tuning-fork.

The pitch of a note depends on the frequency of the sound source. A high-pitched note has a high frequency.

Fig. 2

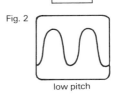
low pitch

high pitch

'Pure' Note   A pure note (a single frequency) is emitted by a tuning-fork and a signal generator connected to a loudspeaker. Generally, notes consist of a main frequency called a *fundamental* mixed with higher frequencies called *overtones*.

Harmonic   A harmonic is a note whose frequency is an exact multiple of the fundamental.

Overtone   An overtone is a harmonic that accompanies the fundamental. It is usually 'weak' compared to the fundamental.

73

Quality　The quality of a note is dictated by the number and strength of the overtones. This explains why a guitar and a violin playing the same note at the same loudness sound different.

Simple Method of Determining the Speed of Sound in Air

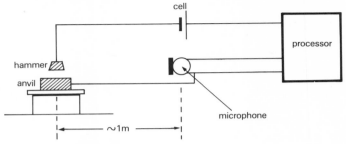

1. Hammer strikes anvil.
2. Processor receives a pulse from cell and a 'clock' in the processor begins to count.
3. A sound wave travels outwards and is picked up by the microphone. It converts sound energy into electrical energy.
4. A voltage-time analog of the incoming sound waves is monitored by the processor.
5. The first peak voltage reading is linked with a later time (recorded by the processor).
6.
$$\text{Speed of sound in air} = \frac{\text{distance travelled}}{\text{time taken}}$$

VELA　Vela is an acronym for Versatile Laboratory Aid and is a single multi-purpose microprocessor-based instrument which can be used in the above experiment.

18 Light and the Electromagnetic Spectrum

Electro-magnetic Spectrum

The electromagnetic (e.m.) spectrum comprises a family of transverse wave-like radiations carrying energy. Light is one of the members of this family.

See overleaf for diagram.

The wavelength λ dictates the colour of the light*. Blue light has a $\lambda \sim 400$ nm whereas red light has a $\lambda \sim 700$ nm. This is the only portion of the e.m. spectrum that we can see. (1 nm = 1 nanometre = 10^{-9} m).

*Strictly speaking, colour resides in the eye-brain system and is not a property of wavelength (see page 84).

Luminous Sources

Luminous sources produce their own light. The Sun, electric lamps and candles are luminous sources.

Non-Luminous Sources

Non-luminous sources do not produce their own light. They rely on luminous sources to reflect light from them in order that we can see them. Most things we see are non-luminous.

Mono-chromatic Waves

Monochromatic waves comprise light waves restricted to a very narrow band of wavelengths – ideally, one wavelength.

Ray of Light

A ray of light defines a specific path along which waves travel, and is perpendicular to a wavefront.

Laws of Reflection

Using a ray-box and a card with a single slit in it we can direct a ray of light at a plane mirror. Having drawn a normal (a perpendicular) to the mirror at the point of incidence we can monitor the path of the reflected ray.

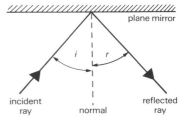

We find:
1. the angle of incidence equals the angle of reflection, $\angle i = \angle r$; and
2. the incident ray, the reflected ray and the normal all lie in the same plane.

These are known as the laws of reflection.

Formation of an Image by a Plane Mirror

Any object can be said to comprise a number of points. Consider one of these points. It could be a luminous point source, or alternatively we can think of light being reflected from it. Let us say we are dealing with a luminous point source. Light from the source will travel in an infinite number

(continues page 77)

75

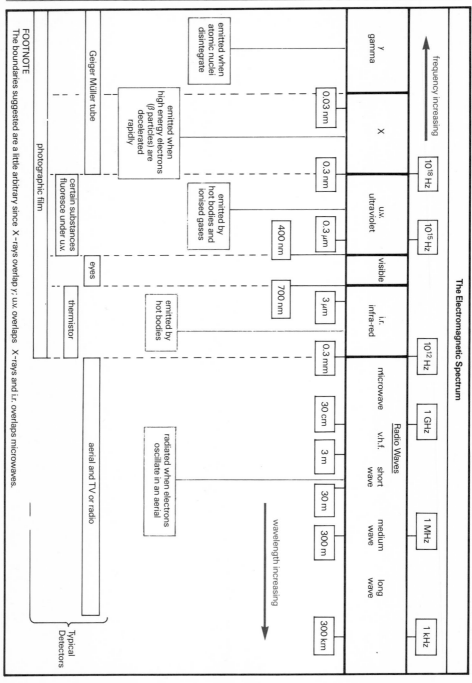

The Electromagnetic Spectrum

frequency increasing

γ gamma		emitted when atomic nuclei disintegrate
X	0.03 nm	emitted when high energy electrons (β particles) are decelerated rapidly
	0.3 nm	
u.v. ultraviolet	0.3 μm	emitted by hot bodies and ionised gases
	400 nm	certain substances fluoresce under u.v.
visible		
i.r. infra-red	700 nm / 3 μm	emitted by hot bodies
microwave	0.3 mm	

10¹⁸ Hz, 10¹⁵ Hz, 10¹² Hz

microwave	1 GHz
v.h.f.	30 cm
short wave	3 m
medium wave	30 m / 300 m
long wave	300 km

Radio Waves

radiated when electrons oscillate in an aerial

wavelength increasing

1 MHz, 1 kHz

Geiger Müller tube

photographic film

eyes

thermistor

aerial and TV or radio

} Typical Detectors

FOOTNOTE
The boundaries suggested are a little arbitrary since X-rays overlap γ, u.v. overlaps X-rays and i.r. overlaps microwaves.

of directions. Place a plane mirror in front of the object and consider two arbitrary directions, i.e. allow two rays from the source to impinge upon the plane mirror.

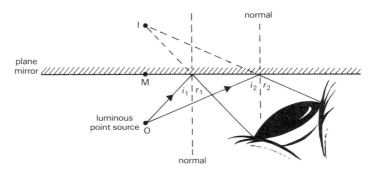

I = image
O = object

The two rays are reflected from the plane mirror according to the laws of reflection. When produced backwards the intersection point locates the image of the object point. In this way we can build an image of an object that comprises more than one point.

OM = IM   The image of an object point in a plane mirror is the same distance behind the mirror as the object is in front.

Virtual Image   I is a *virtual* image of O. The rays of light only appear to come from I. They do not actually intersect in the image. Any ray of light from O will after reflection appear to originate from I. (See page 88 for *real image*.)

Lateral Inversion   A lateral inversion is a sideways reversal of an image. A driver in a car followed by an ambulance will see the word AMBULANCE on looking at the image of it in either his interior mirror or wing mirror because the word has previously been sideways reversed.

Characteristics of an Image Formed by a Plane Mirror
1. Image is as far behind mirror as object is in front.
2. Image is upright.
3. Image is same size as object.
4. Image is virtual.
5. Image is laterally inverted.
6. A point object and image lie on the same normal.

77

Periscope

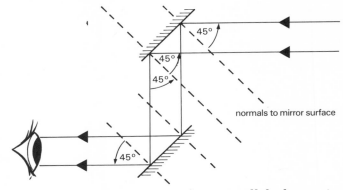

A simple periscope consists of two parallel plane mirrors fixed at 45°.

Use of a Concave Mirror to Focus Light

If an incident parallel beam of light is restricted to being narrow, close to the principal axis of the mirror, then the reflected rays intersect at a single point.

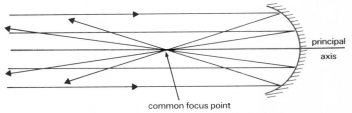

If the mirror were a wide aperture mirror then we would no longer have a common focus point.

Wide Aperture (Diameter) Mirror

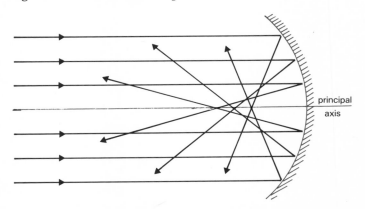

In order to achieve a common focus point with a wide aperture mirror we need to distort it until its shape becomes parabolic.

Parabolic Mirror

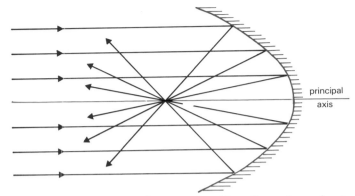

principal axis

Reversibility Principle

The reversibility principle states that if a reflected or refracted (see page 80) ray is reversed in direction it will retrace its original path. It follows that if we were to put a light source at the common focal point of a narrow aperture concave mirror or wide aperture parabolic mirror, then we would finish up with a parallel beam of light as for example, with a searchlight, car headlamp or even a torch. An electric fire often has its heating element(s) placed in front of a reflecting surface in order to maximise the amount of heat energy thrown in a given direction.

Microwaves

Microwaves have frequencies measured in gigahertz (10^9 Hz).

Ionosphere

The ionosphere is a region of the Earth's upper atmosphere which is capable of reflecting radio frequencies. Unfortunately a large proportion of the radiation from outer space is also reflected, creating an obstacle to radio astronomy.

Aerial

An aerial can transmit or receive signals.

Communications Satellites

Communications satellites transmit and receive microwaves. On transmission, a parabolic reflecting surface (dish) concentrates the microwaves into a narrow beam; and, on reception, the dish focuses the microwaves on to the aerial element.

Advantages of Microwaves

1. They pass virtually straight through the ionosphere because of their very high frequency.
2. A high frequency means a greater capability for handling information.

Radio Telescope

A radio telescope has a large steerable parabolic reflector (so that it can be directed at any part of the sky) which focuses weak radio signals from space on to a central receiving aerial at the focus of the paraboloid.

Refraction

When a ray of light impinges upon a transparent medium such as glass, some of the light is reflected according to the laws of reflection, whilst the rest is transmitted. Unless the incident ray is normal to the surface, we find that the direction of the ray inside the medium is different from that of the incident ray. This change of direction or bending of the light is called refraction.

Experiment to Demonstrate Refraction (Glass Block in Air)

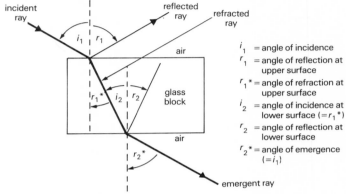

i_1 = angle of incidence
r_1 = angle of reflection at upper surface
$r_1{}^*$ = angle of refraction at upper surface
i_2 = angle of incidence at lower surface $(= r_1{}^*)$
r_2 = angle of reflection at lower surface
$r_2{}^*$ = angle of emergence $(= i_1)$

Semicircular Glass Block

A ray of light passing through the centre of a sphere must meet the surface normally (i.e. at right angles). From the principle of reversibility of light, a point source of light placed at the centre of a sphere must radiate rays in such a way that they meet the surface normally. Similarly, a ray directed towards the centre of a circular glass block must meet the surface normally. No refraction takes place at either surface.

Now bisect the circular block.

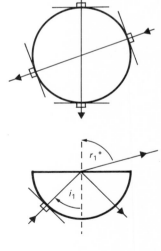

Direct a ray of light towards the centre – the ray must meet the curved surface normally, i.e. no refraction occurs at the curved surface and we can concentrate our attention on the plane surface.

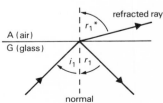

We are moving from an optically dense medium (glass) to an optically rarer medium (air). The light ray is bent (refracted) away from the normal. From the principle of reversibility of light, moving from air to glass would result in the light being bent towards the normal.

Critical Angle and Total Internal Reflection

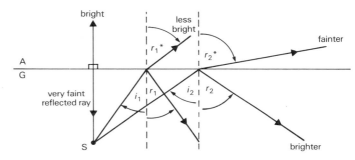

S = luminous point source
As the angle of incidence (*i*) increases, the angle of refraction increases, the refracted ray becoming increasingly faint and the reflected ray increasingly bright. Eventually, the angle of incidence becomes such that the refracted ray (very faint) just escapes, grazing the interface whilst the reflected ray inside the glass is bright.

Critical Angle

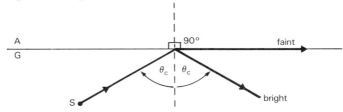

This threshold angle of incidence (θ_c) beyond which total internal reflection takes place (100% reflection) is known as the critical angle.

Total Internal Reflection

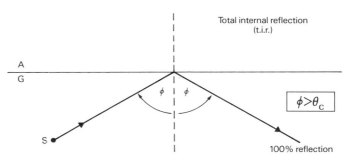

Multiple Images A plane mirror has a finite thickness and as a result several faint images due to partial reflection and refraction accompany a prominent image. The thicker the glass the more widely separated the images.

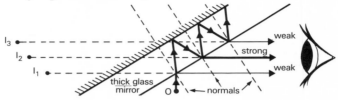

Total Reflecting Prisms Because of multiple or 'ghost' images, high-quality periscopes do not employ plane mirrors but use right-angled isosceles prisms (90°, 45°, 45°).

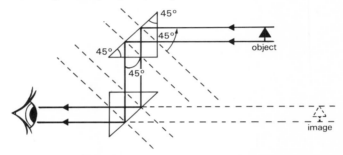

These rays are totally internally reflected because the angle of incidence at the glass/air boundary (45°) is greater than the critical angle between glass and air (42°).

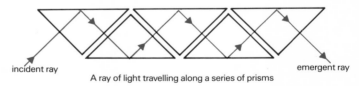

A ray of light travelling along a series of prisms

Optical Fibre

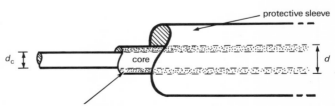

cladding – glass or plastic optically less dense than the core

Core diameter, $d_c \simeq 0.5\,\mu$m
d = diameter of core + cladding $\simeq 125\,\mu$m.

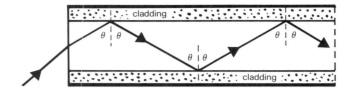

Light from a source impinging upon the core/cladding interface at an angle θ at least equal to the critical angle for this pair of media will be successively totally internally reflected as shown.

Information in the form of a large number of extremely rapid pulses can be sent down a fibre. The light source could be a light-emitting diode (l.e.d.) based on the semiconductor gallium arsenide (GaAs), or a semiconductor laser.

Communica-tions
Optical fibres are increasingly replacing copper wire in the telephone system. Thousands of telephone conversations can be transmitted at the same time by a single fibre. They are also capable of carrying TV pictures and teletext in the form of coded information.

Medicine
Optical fibres are used by doctors to see inside patients' throats, lungs and stomachs. Light is sent down some of the fibres which comprise the bundle, and reflected light from the area of concern is viewed by the doctor through the remainder of the bundle.

Industrial Counter

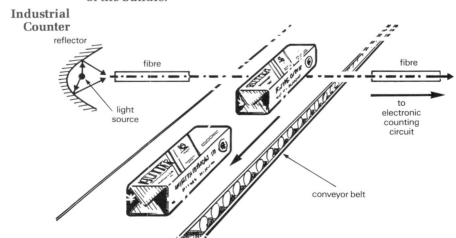

When an object breaks the beam, an electronic counter 'counts'.

Spectrum   Allow a shaft of sunlight to meet a triangular glass prism.

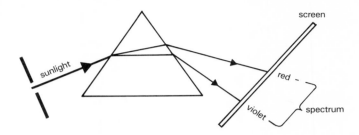

The sunlight (white light) splits up into a band of colours called a spectrum. The splitting of white light into
Dispersion   component colours is called dispersion. The component colours are conventionally identified, Red, Orange, Yellow, Green, Blue, Indigo and Violet (ROY G BIV). (Strictly, there is a very slow gradation of colours from one end to the other.) Dispersion is a result of the different colours travelling with slightly different speeds in the glass.

Colour   Colour is subjective – the colours we see are qualities of our mental image. A person whose colour vision is defective may not be able to discriminate between red and green and so it follows that these colours cannot appear to him or her as they do to a normal observer.

The colour of an object depends on:
1. the nature of the illuminating light;
2. the nature of the surface and surroundings; and
3. the observer.

However, for convenience we assign wavelengths to the colours that a normal observer would perceive.

> Blue light has a wavelength $\sim$ 400 nm
> Red light has a wavelength $\sim$ 700 nm

Visual   The eye is not equally sensitive to the different colours of light
Sensitivity   in the visible spectrum. Visual sensitivity varies with wavelength. The maximum visual effect is obtained with light of wavelength 555 nm (yellow-green).

Brightness   For a given colour (i.e. wavelength) the perceived brightness depends upon the intensity of the wave. This is proportional to the square of its amplitude.

Speed of   The speed of electromagnetic waves in a vacuum is a constant.
Electro-   It is usually given the symbol c, where $c = 3 \times 10^8$ m/s.
magnetic
Waves $c = f \times \lambda$

Radio Waves	If radio waves in the medium waveband have a wavelength of 300 m,

$$\text{then } f = \frac{c}{\lambda} = \frac{3 \times 10^8 \text{ m/s}}{300 \text{ m}} = 10^6/\text{s}, \quad \text{i.e. } f = 1 \text{ MHz.}$$

Electro-magnetic Waves Need No Material Medium for Propagation

Unlike sound waves which cannot travel through a vacuum, e.m. waves can. Think of the e.m. radiation in the form of heat and light reaching the Earth from the Sun. There are 150×10^6 km of near-perfect vacuum between ourselves and the Sun.

Uses of Electro-magnetic Waves:

Microwave Ovens

Microwaves are absorbed by food and liquid. They penetrate ~ 3 cm into the food, after which heat energy is transferred via the mechanism of conduction and convection. The inner walls of a microwave oven are made of metal because microwaves are reflected by metals. A spinning metal paddle reflects the waves in all directions around the oven, and the food is placed on a rotating turntable to ensure uniform cooking.

Radar

Radar is an acronym of Radio Detection And Ranging. Distant objects which cross the path of a directed beam of microwaves reflect the pulses back to the transmitter (which also acts as a receiver). The time taken for a pulse to travel to the object and back enables the distance to the object to be calculated.

Satellites

Microwaves are used in satellite communication (see also Solar Power Station, page 65).

X-Rays

1. Short wavelength X-rays are used in hospitals to kill cancer cells.
2. Less penetrating (longer wavelength) X-rays penetrate flesh but not bone and are used in dental X-ray photography. Hidden faults inside metal castings can be located using X-ray photography.

Infra-red

1. Infra-red (i.r.) photographs can detect poor blood circulation.
2. In warfare the i.r. emitted from the hot engine of an aircraft can be tracked.
3. Infra-red photographs can be taken in the dark. The image formed by a thermal imaging camera is initially in shades of grey. A computer assigns a colour to each shade, resulting in a colour picture. Such cameras can detect temperature differences as small as 0.1°C.
4. The remote control of TV and video uses i.r.

Ultraviolet
1. Ultraviolet (u.v.) radiation is what produces a sun-tan.
2. The coated inner surface of fluorescent tubes radiates visible light when u.v. (emitted by mercury vapour inside the tube) impinges.
3. Clothes washed in detergents fluoresce in sunlight as a result of the u.v. which the sunlight contains.

Light Detection and Ranging (LIDAR)
Laser light in the form of a narrow collimated (parallel) beam is increasingly being used as a range-finder by the armed forces. The system consists of a pulsed laser, a telescope (to collect the reflected light), a photodetector and an accurate timer. The Apollo space missions left *retroreflectors* on the surface of the Moon, and the distance to the Moon has been measured using this technique.

Convex Lens, Positive Lens, Plus Lens, Converging Lens
The four terms on the left are alternative ways of describing a lens that is thick in the middle and thin around the edge. The centre of the lens is known as the *optical centre* C, and a line through C at right angles to the lens is known as the *principal axis*.

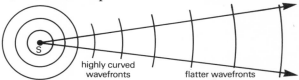

We can think of reflected light from a non-luminous point object S radiating out as a series of spherical waves. In two dimensions we can represent these waves as circles.

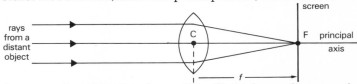

The diagram suggests that the wavefronts impinging upon a convex lens from a distant object will be plane, i.e. rays emanating from the object will be parallel.

Principal Focus, Focal Length
When a beam of light parallel to the principal axis passes through a convex lens it is refracted so as to converge to a point on the axis called the *principal focus*, labelled F. The distance CF is called the *focal length* of the lens. Since light can fall on either face of a lens, it has two principal foci, one on each side.

A screen placed in the plane of F will catch a real image of a distant object.

Rays Used in Image Construction

1. A ray of light parallel to the principal axis of a convex lens is refracted through a principal focus.
2. A ray of light passing through the optical centre is undeviated.
3. A ray passing through a principal focus is refracted parallel to the principal axis.

Usually only rays *1* and *2* are required to locate the image of an object.

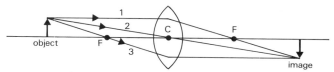

Simple Camera

A camera is a light-tight box in which a convex lens forms a real image on a film at the back of the box. The lens is not movable and any object further than about 2 metres from the camera is effectively at infinity relative to the camera dimensions. The area of the lens receiving light can be changed by introducing a variable aperture (hole) either in front of or behind the lens. The aperture can be made small for a bright scene or large for a dull one.

Stop

The device that controls the aperture area is known as a *stop*.

f-Numbers

The diameter of the aperture is expressed as a fraction of the focal length and so *f*-16 is one sixteenth of the focal length whereas *f*-4 is one quarter of the focal length. The *smaller* the *f*-number, the *larger* the aperture.

Exposure Time

The exposure time is controlled by a shutter which opens for a pre-set time (usually variable), allowing light to reach the film. A fast-moving object would require a small exposure time and a small *f*-number.

Simple Camera Schematic

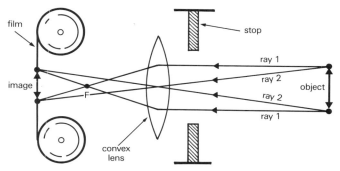

In this schematic, the light-tight box and the shutter are not shown.

Any object can be considered to be made up from an infinite number of object points. The images of the two extreme object points have been located using construction rays *1* and *2*.

Note, that the image here is:

1. diminished;
2. inverted; and
3. real, i.e. it has been formed by the intersection of real rays.

Real Image A real image is one that can be projected on to a screen.

Using a Single Convex Lens as a Projection Lens

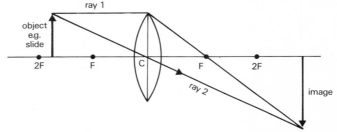

2F is a point on the principal axis a distance twice the focal length from C.

The image is:

1. magnified;
2. inverted – if the slide is turned upside-down, the image of it will appear the right way up; and
3. real.

The size of the image can be changed by changing the slide/lens distance.

Using a Convex Lens as a Magnifying Glass Place an object (e.g. print on a page) between F and C.

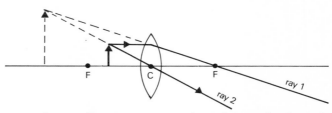

Rays *1* and *2* are divergent. We produce the rays backwards to locate the image.

The image is:

1. magnified;
2. upright; and
3. virtual, i.e. the rays of light only appear to come from it.

Virtual Image A virtual image is one that cannot be formed on a screen.

19 Electricity

Conductor A conductor is a substance which readily allows electrons to flow through it. Silver and copper are especially good conductors.

Insulator An insulator is a substance which does not readily allow electrons to flow through it. Most non-metals are good insulators. Dry air, glass, rubber, porcelain and plastics such as polythene are good insulators.

Charging by Rubbing If a strip of polythene is rubbed with dry wool, electrons are transferred from the cloth to the polythene, leaving the polythene negatively charged. Rubbing a perspex rod with dry wool transfers electrons from the perspex to the cloth, leaving the perspex positively charged. Prior to rubbing, the polythene and the perspex are electrically neutral. Materials which are positively charged have a deficiency of electrons.

Like Charges Repel

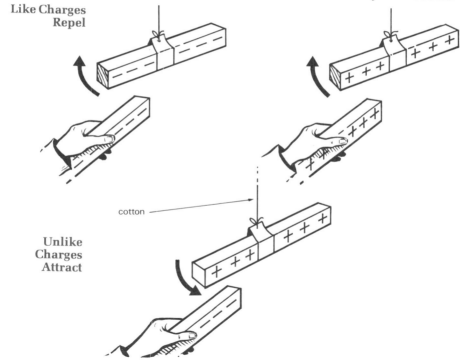

cotton

Unlike Charges Attract

Electrostatic Attraction Electrostatic attraction is the attraction that opposite electrical charges have for each other.

Charged Objects Attract Uncharged Objects

A plastic comb which has been pulled through your hair becomes charged and is capable of picking up tiny scraps of paper. If the comb is negatively charged, electrons in the atoms of the paper redistribute themselves so that the paper facing the comb is effectively in deficit of negative charge (i.e. positively charged) and attraction takes place.

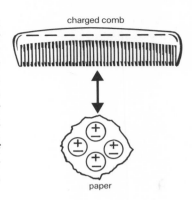

Paper is an insulator. There are no free electrons in paper.

Similarly, pulling out a plastic record from a paper sleeve charges the record. Dust is an insulator and dust particles redistribute their electron concentration so that they are attracted to the record. Charges are said to be induced in the paper or the dust.

Electrostatic Precipitation

Electrostatic precipitation is a means of controlling the pollution of air. Effluent gases that would normally pollute the atmosphere are subjected to an electrostatic field which is provided by a series of overlapping positive and negative electrodes. Depending upon the type of pollutant, solid or liquid particles suspended in the gas are attracted to one or other of the sets of electrodes.

Metallic Conductor

A metallic conductor can be thought of as a highly structured array of ions in a sea of electrons. The free electrons move randomly.

Current Flow

A current flow consists of a bulk drift of electrons moving randomly in one direction.

Electric Current

An electric current consists of moving electric charges – namely electrons.

Primary Cell

A primary cell is a device which maintains (by chemical action) a surplus of electrons at one terminal (the negative) and a deficit at the other (the positive). A continuous current flow can be maintained if:

1. there is a complete circuit through which current can flow; and

2. the circuit contains a device which maintains a difference in the state of charges between its terminals (e.g. a primary cell).

Secondary Cell A secondary cell is one that can be recharged by passing a current through it in the opposite direction to which it would normally discharge.

Semi-conductor A semiconductor (s.c.) is a material having an electrical conductivity between that of insulators and metallic conductors. The resistance of a s.c. decreases with increasing temperature and the presence of impurities. Typical s.c.'s include germanium, silicon, selenium and lead telluride.

Direct Current A direct current (d.c.) is an electric current which always flows in the same direction.

Alternating Current An alternating current (a.c.) reaches a maximum in one direction, decreases, eventually reverses and reaches a maximum in the opposite direction.

This cycle is continuously repeated.

Frequency of an Alternating Current The frequency of an a.c. is the number of cycles per second. Three cycles are shown below. The frequency of the mains (operating at 240 V) is 50 cycles per second or 50 hertz (50 Hz).

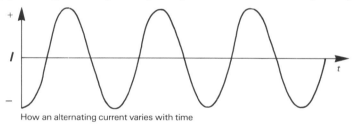

How an alternating current varies with time

Units of Electrical Current The ampere (A) is the S.I. unit of electrical current.

Units of Electrical Charge The coulomb (C) is the unit of electrical charge. It is equal to the charge on about 6×10^{18} electrons. (The charge on one electron is far too small for practical purposes.) The coulomb is defined in terms of the ampere – it is that amount of charge passing any point in a circuit when a steady current of 1 ampere flows for 1 second. Mathematically we can describe the relationship between the charge in coulombs and electrical current in amperes as follows:

$$Q = I \times t$$

where Q = charge in coulombs,
I = electrical current in amperes, and
t = time in seconds.

A charge of 6C would pass each point in 3 s if the current was 2 A (i.e. $I \times t = 2 \times 3 = 6$).

91

Standard Symbols for Electrical Components

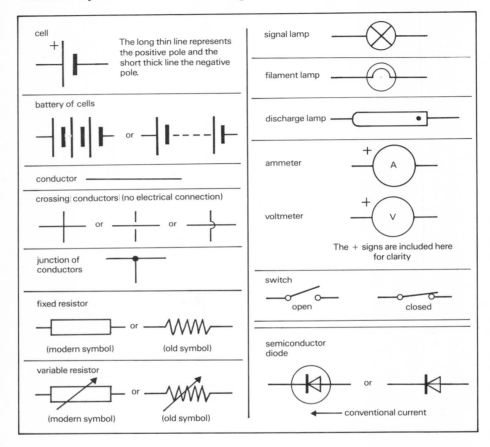

cell — The long thin line represents the positive pole and the short thick line the negative pole.

battery of cells

conductor

crossing conductors (no electrical connection)

junction of conductors

fixed resistor — (modern symbol) — (old symbol)

variable resistor — (modern symbol) — (old symbol)

signal lamp

filament lamp

discharge lamp

ammeter

voltmeter

The + signs are included here for clarity

switch — open — closed

semiconductor diode — conventional current

Conventional Current Flow

Prior to the discovery of the electron, scientists *agreed* to think of electrical current flowing around a circuit in the direction in which positive charges would flow, i.e. in the direction from positive to negative of a battery. This is referred to as *conventional current flow* and the agreement still holds.

Consider this simple circuit comprising a cell and a lamp.

The electrons actually flow from the negative terminal of the supply to the positive terminal whereas conventional current flow is in the opposite sense.

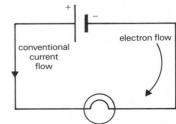

conventional current flow

electron flow

Potential Difference

Earlier we recognised the existence of the Earth's gravitational field wherein different locations above ground possess different potentials, depending on the level above the ground. We defined the potential difference (p.d.) between two points as the energy released per kg when an object falls from one point to another.

An analogous situation occurs in electricity but now we must think in terms of electron movement. A battery has a p.d. across its terminals. Joining a conductor across the terminals results in positive charge moving (if it could) from the positive to the negative terminal – or (what amounts to the same thing) negative charges (electrons) moving from the negative to the positive terminal. Connecting a lamp across the terminals results in electrons moving through the filament releasing energy in the form of light and heat.

The Volt

The volt is defined to be that p.d. between two points in a circuit if 1 joule of electrical energy is converted into other forms of energy (e.g. light and heat) when 1 coulomb passes from one point to the other:

1 volt	= 1 joule per coulomb
2 volts	= 2 joules per coulomb
10 volts	= 10 joules per coulomb

If we represent the p.d. by V, the energy changed (i.e. the work done) by W, and the charge in coulombs by Q we can write:

$$V = \frac{W}{Q}$$ i.e. Potential difference $= \dfrac{\text{Work done}}{\text{Charge moved}}$

or, rearranging:

$$W = V \times Q$$

Also, if Q is in the form of a steady current I (amperes) flowing for a time t (seconds), then since $Q = I \times t$:

$$W = I \times t \times V$$

Measuring Current

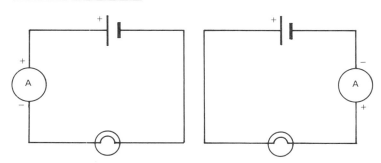

An ammeter is an instrument for measuring electric current.

1. The ammeter should be connected *in series*.
2. The ammeter *must* be connected in the circuit in such a way that its positive terminal should be connected to the positive terminal of the supply irrespective of the number of components between the ammeter and the battery.
3. Ammeters have a very low resistance. The *perfect* ammeter would absorb no energy. The p.d. across it would be zero.

Cells and Batteries

Strictly, a group of cells connected together is called a battery.

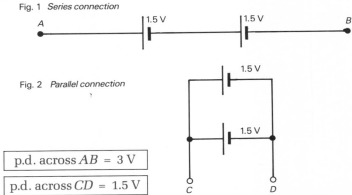

Fig. 1 *Series connection*

Fig. 2 *Parallel connection*

p.d. across AB = 3 V

p.d. across CD = 1.5 V

The arrangement in fig. 2 behaves as a larger cell, has a longer life, and allows us to draw a larger current. To avoid the possibility of discharge due to current circulating in the battery itself, it is prudent after use to disconnect such a combination.

Measuring Potential Difference

A voltmeter is an instrument for measuring p.d. Unlike an ammeter which is connected *in series* in a circuit, a voltmeter is connected *across* that part of the circuit where the p.d. is required.

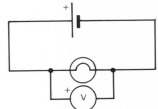

1. The voltmeter is connected *in parallel.*
2. Voltmeters (like ammeters) have to be connected into the circuit in such a way that the positive terminal should be connected to the positive terminal of the supply irrespective of the number of components between the voltmeter and the supply.
3. Voltmeters should have a very high resistance. The *perfect* voltmeter should take no current and absorb no energy, i.e. it should have an infinite resistance.

Resistance (R) The size of the opposition of the atomic structure of a substance to the flow of electrons is called its resistance (R). Insulators strongly oppose the movement of electrons whereas conductors offer little opposition.

Units of Resistance The unit of resistance is the ohm (Ω). This is the resistance of a conductor which is such that a p.d. of 1 volt applied across it produces a current flow of 1 ampere through it. Hence $R = \dfrac{V}{I}$.

Consider a cylindrical copper wire (*kept at a constant temperature*) of length *l* and cross-sectional area A. The resistance is directly proportional to the length of the conductor:

$$R \propto l$$

Keeping the length of copper wire constant and doubling the cross-sectional area (at constant temperature) halves the resistance to electron flow. Trebling the cross-sectional area reduces the resistance encountered by a factor of three. The resistance is said to be inversely proportional to the cross-sectional area:

$$R \propto \frac{1}{A}$$ (N.B. $A = \dfrac{\pi d^2}{4}$ where d = wire diameter)

Resistance Varies with Temperature An increase of temperature increases the resistance of most metals. You can think of the atoms within a metal gaining energy with increasing temperature, resulting in an overall increase in amplitude and rate of vibration, thus making it more difficult for the electrons to flow.

The resistance of non-metals, carbon and most semi-conductor materials decreases with increasing temperature. Certain alloys such as constantan and manganin are unusual in that their resistance is reasonably constant over a wide temperature variation.

Ohm's Law The size of the electrical current through a conductor is directly proportional to the applied p.d. across its ends *if the temperature is constant*. For a constant p.d. *V*, if *I* decreases, it follows that *R* increases; and if *I* increases, *R* decreases. For most metallic conductors at constant temperature, *V/I* always has the same value when *V* is varied and the corresponding value of *I* found. Doubling *V* doubles *I*, trebling *V* trebles *I* and so on. Thus $\dfrac{V}{I} = R$. This is Ohm's Law. We can express Ohm's law in two other ways.

$$I = \frac{V}{R} \quad \text{or} \quad V = I \times R$$

If *V* is in volts, and *I* is in amps, then *R* is in ohms.

Ohmic Components	Ohmic components are components that obey Ohm's Law. Most metals, certain alloys and electrolytic (conducting) solutions obey Ohm's law.

Non-Ohmic or Non-Linear Components	Non-ohmic components are components that do not obey Ohm's Law. Transistors, thermistors, valves and semiconductor diodes do not obey Ohm's Law, or obey Ohm's Law only over certain specified ranges of applied potential difference.

Resistors in Series

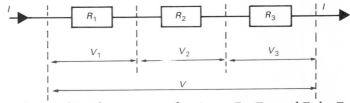

Let the combined resistance of resistors R_1, R_2, and R_3 be R. The same current flows through each resistor. Let this current be I. The total p.d. V across all three is equal to the sum of the separate p.d.'s across them, i.e.

$$V = V_1 + V_2 + V_3$$
$$IR = IR_1 + IR_2 + IR_3$$

Thus: $\boxed{R = R_1 + R_2 + R_3}$

Use of $R = R_1 + R_2 + R_3$ If $R_1 = 3\,\Omega$, $R_2 = 5\,\Omega$ and $R_3 = 2\,\Omega$, then $R = 10\,\Omega$.

Resistors in Parallel

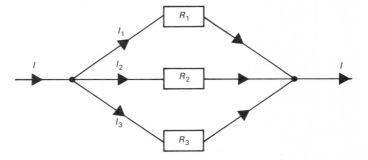

The sum of the currents in the branches of a parallel circuit is equal to the current entering or leaving the parallel section:

$$I = I_1 + I_2 + I_3$$

The p.d. between the ends of each resistor is the same. Let us label this p.d. V.

So, $I_1 = \dfrac{V}{R_1}$ $I_2 = \dfrac{V}{R_2}$ $I_3 = \dfrac{V}{R_3}$

Let R be the combined resistance.

Since $I = \dfrac{V}{R}$, then: $\dfrac{V}{R} = \dfrac{V}{R_1} + \dfrac{V}{R_2} + \dfrac{V}{R_3}$

Thus:
$$\frac{1}{R} = \frac{1}{R_1} + \frac{1}{R_2} + \frac{1}{R_3}$$

Use of
$\dfrac{1}{R} = \dfrac{1}{R_1} + \dfrac{1}{R_2} + \dfrac{1}{R_3}$

If $R_1 = 3\,\Omega$, $R_2 = 5\,\Omega$ and $R_3 = 6\,\Omega$,

then: $\dfrac{1}{R} = \dfrac{1}{3} + \dfrac{1}{5} + \dfrac{1}{6} = \dfrac{10}{30} + \dfrac{6}{30} + \dfrac{5}{30} = \dfrac{21}{30}$

$\therefore R = \dfrac{30}{21} = 1.43\,\Omega$

Useful Multiples and Sub-Multiples of Basic Electrical Units

Current (I)	Voltage (V)	Resistance (R)
1 ampere = 1 A	1 volt = 1 V	1 ohm = 1 Ω
1 milliamp = 1 mA = 10^{-3} A	1 millivolt = 1 mV	1 kilohm = 1 kΩ = $10^3\,\Omega$
1 microamp = 1 μA = 10^{-6} A	1 microvolt = 1 μV	1 megohm = 1 MΩ = $10^6\,\Omega$
	1 kilovolt = 1 kV = 10^3V	

N.B. $10^{-3} = \dfrac{1}{1000}$, and $10^3 = 1000$; $10^{-6} = \dfrac{1}{1\,000\,000}$, and $10^6 = 1\,000\,000$

Terminal Potential Difference

The terminal p.d. of a cell is the reading on a voltmeter connected across the cell terminals.

Open Circuit

Open circuit terminal p.d. is the reading obtained when the cell is not supplying current to any component(s).

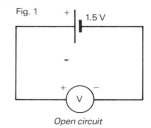

Fig. 1

1.5 V

Open circuit

voltmeter reading = 1.5 V

Closed Circuit

Closed circuit terminal p.d. is the reading obtained when the cell is supplying current to other component(s) connected to it.

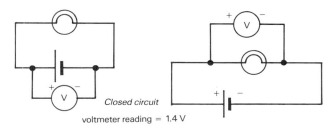

Fig. 2

Closed circuit

voltmeter reading = 1.4 V

Potential Difference

The terminal p.d. on closed circuit (see fig. 2) is the p.d. applied to the lamp, i.e. 1.4 V in our example.

Closed circuit terminal p.d. can be regarded as the number of joules of electrical energy *changed* per coulomb in the external circuit. In fig. 2, 1.4 J of electrical energy is changed into heat and light per coulomb.

Open circuit terminal p.d. is the number of joules of electrical energy a cell or battery gives to each coulomb. If a battery gives 1.5 J of electrical energy to each coulomb on open circuit we say it has an electromotive force (e.m.f.) of 1.5 V.

Electro-
motive
Force

Electromotive force (e.m.f.) measures *energy* per coulomb. (The term is misleading since we might expect it to measure force per coulomb!) The e.m.f. of a cell or battery (or other electrical energy source) is its terminal p.d. on open circuit.

'Lost' Energy
per Coulomb

The lost energy per coulomb is due to the cell having resistance (internal resistance). Each coulomb wastes 0.1 J (in our example) in order to get through the cell itself.

Internal
Resistance

The internal resistance of a cell is labelled r.

Ohm's Law
Applied to
Complete
Circuits

The energy supplied per coulomb by cell or battery is equal to the energy changed into other forms (e.g. heat and light) in the external circuit plus the energy wasted per coulomb on cell resistance.

$$\boxed{\text{e.m.f.} = \text{useful p.d.} + \text{'lost' p.d.}}$$

The e.m.f. of an electrical energy source can be regarded as the sum total of the p.d.'s which it can produce across all the various components of a circuit, including the p.d. required to drive the current through the cell itself.

Circuit
Equation

$$E = V + v$$

e.m.f. of cell   terminal p.d. on closed circuit   lost p.d.

which may also be written: $\boxed{E = IR + Ir = I(R + r)}$

where R is the total equivalent resistance of any resistive components in the external circuit, and r is the internal resistance of the cell.

Example
Problem

A cell of e.m.f. 1.5 V and internal resistance 1 Ω is connected to a resistor of 5 Ω. Find the current in the circuit.

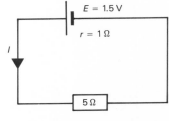

Solution

Using: $E = I(R + r)$
$1.5 = I(5 + 1) = I(6)$
$\therefore I = \dfrac{1.5}{6.0} = \dfrac{1}{4} = 0.25\ \text{A}$

Experiment to Determine Resistance by Use of Voltmeter-Ammeter Readings

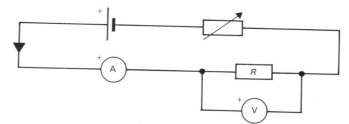

1. The current through R is measured by the ammeter.
2. The p.d. across R is measured by the voltmeter.
3. For a given setting of the variable resistor, the ratio of V to I gives R, i.e. $R = \dfrac{V}{I}$
4. Changing the size of the variable resistor alters both I and V. However, $\left(\dfrac{V}{I}\right)$ will be a constant if the temperature is constant.

V/I and I/V Graphs for a Metal at Constant Temperature

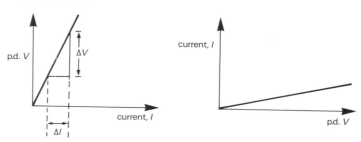

The slope of the V/I graph, $\left(\dfrac{\Delta V}{\Delta I}\right)$, yields R.

Characteristic Curve

However, it is usual to plot the value of I resulting from an applied p.d., V, as shown in the second graph. This form of graph for any device is called a *characteristic curve* and will be used from now on.

Characteristic Curve for a Filament Lamp

Provided I is low (low temperature), the ratio of V to I is constant. But as the temperature increases (I increases), V increases more rapidly than I so that $\dfrac{V}{I}(=R)$ increases. As the lamp filament gets hotter its resistance increases. (The reciprocal of the slope of an I/V graph yields R.)

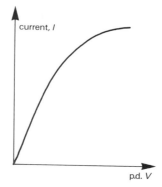

Characteristic Curve for a Semiconductor Diode
A diode permits a current to flow (to any extent) *only one way*. When connected in this way in a circuit it is said to be *forward biased*. When the diode is connected in the opposite sense it is said to be *reverse biased*. Virtually no current flows through the diode when reverse biased.

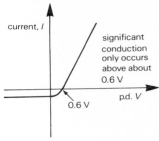

Characteristic Curve for a Thermistor
The characteristic curve denotes a thermistor whose resistance *decreases* with *increasing* temperature.

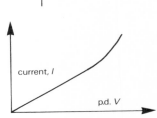

$P = I \times V$
Earlier we saw that an electric lamp converts electrical energy (in joules) to heat energy and light energy. The change in electrical energy, $W = I \times t \times V$. Dividing both sides of this equation by t tells us that the electrical energy changed per second $\left(\dfrac{W}{t}\right)$ into heat and light equals $I \times V$.

Power is defined to be the rate of energy conversion.

Power P (in watts)	=	current I (in amps)	×	p.d. V (in volts)

The Kilowatt-Hour (kWh)
The kilowatt-hour is a unit of energy. It is the energy supplied when a rate of working of 1 kilowatt is maintained for 1 hour. Electricity meters are marked in kWh. The amount of energy used in kWh equals the power (in kW) × time (in hours).

Example Problem
A 3-kW immersion heater is used for 10 hours at a cost of 5p per kilowatt-hour. The heater is designed for use on 240 V mains. Find (a) the current taken from the mains;

  (b) the resistance of the heater;

  (c) the energy used in 1 hour;

  (d) the cost of using the heater for 6 hours.

Solution

(a) $P = 3\,\text{kW} = 3000\,\text{W}$
$P = V \times I$
$3000 = 240 \times I$
$I = \dfrac{3000}{240} = 12.5\,\text{A}$

(b) $V = I \times R$
$R = \dfrac{V}{I}$
$R = \dfrac{240}{12.5} = 19.2\,\Omega$

(c)   3 kW = 3000 W, and 1 W = 1 J/s
∴ 3000 W = 3000 J/s
3600 s = 1 hour
∴ Energy used in 1 hour = 3000 × 3600 J
= 10 800 000 W = 10.8 MW

(d)   Number of kWh = 3 × 6 = 18 kWh
Cost at 5p per kWh = 90p

Symbol for a Fuse

(modern symbol)   (old symbol)

Fuse A fuse consists of a short length of metal wire of low melting-point (tin or tinned copper). When the current exceeds a particular value the fuse wire melts or blows and breaks the circuit. Incorporating a fuse minimises the risk of (i) fire owing to the wiring overheating, and (ii) damage to appliances.

A 2-kW fire used at 240 V draws 8.33 A. A 5A fuse plugged into the circuit will blow, break the circuit and protect the wiring. If the live wire makes contact with neutral or touches a part of the equipment that is earthed, an extra large current flows through the wiring and the fuse blows.

M.C.B.'s. These are Miniature Circuit Breakers which switch the circuit off if the current exceeds a particular value. They can be used instead of fuses.

E.L.C.B.'s. Earth Leakage Circuit Breakers.

R.C.C.B.'s. Residual Current Circuit Breakers.

R.C.D.'s. Residual Current Devices.

These continuously check that the amount of current flowing along the live wire is matched by the return flow along the neutral wire. Any imbalance (current escaping) results in an automatic current cut-off. (N.B. These imbalances may not be big enough to blow a fuse or trip an M.C.B.)

R.C.C.B. units fitted into modern consumer units protect the whole electrical system of a household, or outlets incorporating R.C.C.B. can replace conventional socket outlets. Outdoor appliances including lawn mowers, hedge trimmers and power tools should not be used without R.C.C.B. protection.

Electric Cables Electric cables are also rated for the current they can pass. The rating is lower for a completely coiled cable than when the cable is unwound since the heat energy produced disperses more slowly.

101

Simplified House Wiring Diagram

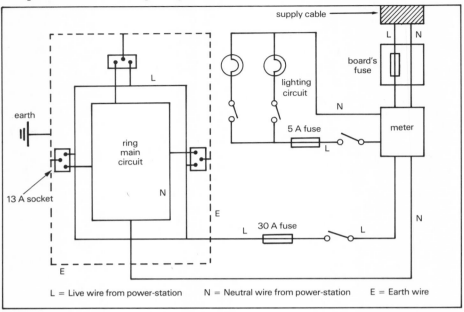

L = Live wire from power-station   N = Neutral wire from power-station   E = Earth wire

Ring Main   The ring main is a cable comprising live, neutral and earth wires each forming a 'ring' around the house. Both the live and neutral wires carry current but the neutral is earthed at a local sub-station and is at zero potential. The ring main is protected by a 30 A fuse and each power point is protected by a fuse inside the plug.

The ring mains fuse restricts the amount of power that can be drawn from it. It can supply only 7200 watts (7.2 kW) at any time. ($P = V \times I = 240\,\text{V} \times 30\,\text{A} = 7200\,\text{W}$).

If the ring is overloaded, the mains fuse blows and there is no further supply to any sockets. In modern house wiring systems, before the fuse blows, a switch is tripped to break the circuit so the fuse doesn't have to be replaced.

Advantage of Domestic Ring Main   Thinner cable can be used, since current to each socket flows by two paths.

Lighting Circuit   The lighting circuit is protected by a 5A fuse.

Earth Wire   The earth wire is connected to a *metal* water pipe in the house or to a supply cable earth. The earth wire *only* carries current if there is a fault. If a live wire touches the metal case of an appliance (which has little resistance), a large current flows through the fuse (in the live wire) to earth via the earth pin on a three-pin plug which is connected to the case. The fuse blows and the appliance is turned off until the fault can be rectified. If there were no earth connection, anyone touching the case might receive a *fatal* electric shock, since the current would then flow through that person to earth.

Switches and Fuses

Switches and fuses are found solely in the *live wire*. Inserting them into the *neutral wire* (at the lower potential) would mean that lamp and power sockets would be potentially lethal even when switches were turned to *off* or after fuses had blown.

Threshold of Muscular Decontrol

The threshold of muscular decontrol is about 15 mA 50 Hz a.c. and 70 mA d.c. Severe muscular contractions make it difficult for the casualty to release his/her hold. An increase in current beyond 20 mA 50 Hz a.c. or 80 mA d.c. can be fatal. The electrical resistance of the body (which governs the size of the current) varies from a few hundred ohms to thousands of ohms and depends on whether the skin is moist or dry.

Fuse Ratings

The rule is always to use a fuse of the lowest possible value that will still allow the current drawn by the appliance to flow.

Examples of How to Work Out the Correct Fuse Value

1. Electric Iron (600 W)

   Supply Voltage = 240 V

   $P = V \times I$

   $I = 2.5$ A

   Therefore, use a 3 A fuse (rather than a 5 A or 13 A fuse).

   Generally, appliances rated at <720 W require a 3 A fuse (coloured red), unless a high starting current is required (e.g. a spin-drier or vacuum cleaner), in which case the manufacturer's instructions should be followed.

2. Immersion Heater (3 kW = 3000 W)

   Supply Voltage = 240 V

   $P = V \times I$

   $I = 12.5$ A

   Therefore, use a 13A fuse.

Colour Code

The colour code specified has the advantage of being distinguishable by people who are red/green colour-blind.

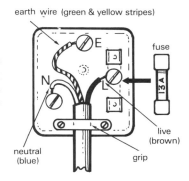

earth wire (green & yellow stripes)

fuse

live (brown)

neutral (blue)

grip

How to Wire a Fused Three Pin Plug

1. Slit outer sheath of flex with a sharp knife.
2. Strip insulating plastic from the three wires. Twist the strands of each wire together. Trim to correct length.
3. *For pillar terminal plugs*
   For small diameter wires fold the bared ends back to double them up. Push each wire into its appropriate terminal and screw down tightly allowing as much slack as possible for the earth conductor. (If the flex is pulled from the plug, the earth wire must be the last to disconnect should the grip fail.)

pillar terminal

   For stud terminal plugs
   Twist the bare threads of each wire into a clockwise loop. Screw the trimmed wires firmly around the appropriate terminals. Ensure the wires are trapped under the washers whilst tightening the studs.

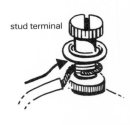

stud terminal

4. Check that the fuse is of the correct rating for the appliance.
5. Fix flex firmly in grip.
6. Ensure there are no loose strands of wire within the plug. These could cause short circuits.
7. Replace plug top.

Electrical Energy Is Transmitted at High Voltage

Electrical energy is transmitted at high voltage because this gives a greatly reduced power loss (as heat) in communicating cables.

Power Lost as Heat in a Cable

Power lost as heat in a cable can be calculated using:

$$P = I^2R$$

where P = heat energy lost per second
R = resistance of the cable, and
I = current transmitted in amps.

Imagine we wish to transmit 5 kW (5000 W) of power through a cable of resistance 5 Ω.
We could transmit, for example, 1 A at 5000 V or 100 A at 50 V. In the first case the power loss would be 5 W and in the second 50 kW!

20 Magnetism and Electromagnetism

Lodestone (Fe_3O_4)	A lodestone (magnetic iron oxide) is a natural magnet. When freely suspended it points North-South.
Magnetic Substances (Ferro-magnetic)	Magnetic substances are substances that attract other metals or other magnets. They include iron, cobalt and nickel, and alloys such as steel, and also alloys of other metals which, on their own, are not magnetic.
Magnetically Hard Material	A hard magnetic material is one that is difficult to magnetise (low susceptibility) but retains its magnetism well (high retentivity), e.g. steel.
Magnetically Soft Material	A soft magnetic material is one that is easily magnetised (high susceptibility) but retains little magnetism on removing the magnetising field (low retentivity), e.g. iron.
Permanent Magnets	Permanent magnets are formed from magnetically hard material, and are usually horseshoe-shaped or in the form of a rectangular bar.
Freely Suspended Bar Magnet	A freely suspended bar magnet aligns with the Earth's magnetic field.
North-Seeking Pole (North Pole)	The North-seeking pole is the end of a magnet which points approximately geographic North. The other end is called the south pole. The attracting power of a magnet is greatest at its poles.
Like Poles Repel	Two N or two S poles repel.
Unlike Poles Attract	A N and a S pole attract.
Compass	A compass consists of a magnetised needle pivoted at its centre.
Un-magnetised Material	An unmagnetised material is attracted to *both* poles of a magnet.
Attraction and Repulsion	Let both poles of a permanent magnet be brought in turn near to one pole of a suspended magnet. We should observe attraction and repulsion. Repulsion is the only sure way of discovering whether an object is a magnet or not.
Magnetic Field	A magnetic field is a force field surrounding a magnet. It can also be found in the vicinity of a conductor through which current is flowing.

105

Magnetic Domain

A magnetic domain is a region in a ferromagnetic material where each atom can be thought of as a tiny magnet and all atoms in the region point in the same direction. A magnet comprises many domains. In a magnetised steel bar all the domains line up in approximately the same direction.

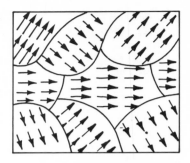

Strength of a Magnet

The strength of a magnet is determined by how well the domains are lined up.

Magnetic Induction Precedes Attraction

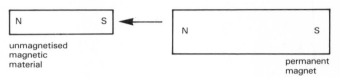

An unmagnetised magnetic material has magnetism induced in it as a consequence of being brought into the vicinity of a magnetic field. In the above diagram the magnetic field is provided by the permanent magnet. Note the polarity of the unmagnetised material.

The Earth's Magnetic Field

The Earth's magnetic field can be thought of as being provided by a giant bar magnet within the Earth whose S pole points magnetic North.

Angle of Declination

The angle of declination is the angle between magnetic North and true geographic North.

Direction of a Magnetic Field

The direction of a magnetic field is the direction in which the N pole of a plotting compass points.

Lines of Magnetic Force (Flux) around a Bar Magnet

Lines of flux can be mapped with a plotting compass.

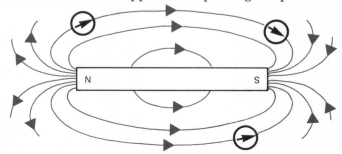

Magnetic Shielding
Magnetic shielding of electrical devices that could be adversely affected by stray or unwanted magnetic fields is achieved by surrounding the device in a soft iron container.

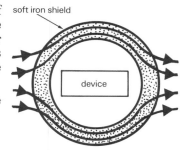

Lines of magnetic force concentrate in the soft iron.

Making a Magnet:

By Stroking
One pole of a permanent magnet is used to stroke a steel knitting-needle, for example, end to end in the same direction.

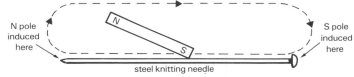

The magnet must be raised well above the steel at the end of each stroke. The polarity of the end of the steel where the magnetising pole leaves is opposite in polarity to the magnetising pole.

By Magnetic Induction
In magnetic induction, a magnetic pole induces an unlike pole near to it and a like pole away from it.

Using a Solenoid
A solenoid is a cylindrical coil of insulated copper wire.
1. Place steel rod in solenoid.
2. Connect solenoid to low-voltage *d.c.* supply.
3. Briefly switch current on. Switch off.
The steel rod is now a magnet.

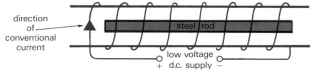

The polarity of the magnet depends on the direction of the current. View one end of the solenoid end-on.

If the conventional current in the coil, when viewed *externally*, is flowing aNticlockwise that end of the enclosed rod becomes a N pole. If current flows clockwiSe, then the end becomes a S pole.

107

Demagnetising a Magnet

Demagnetising a magnet involves placing it inside a solenoid through which *a.c.* is flowing. The magnet is very slowly moved a few metres from the solenoid. The solenoid is placed with its axis pointing East-West.

Electric Current Produces a Magnetic Field

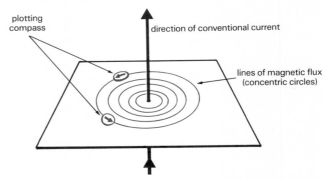

plotting compass

direction of conventional current

lines of magnetic flux (concentric circles)

Field due to a Straight Wire

A plotting compass or compasses can map out the direction of the field at different points.

The Right-Hand Screw Rule

The right-hand screw rule predicts the direction of the field. The direction of rotation of a right-handed screw moved in the direction of conventional current flow gives the field direction.

Field due to a Solenoid

The field due to a solenoid is similar to that of a bar magnet.

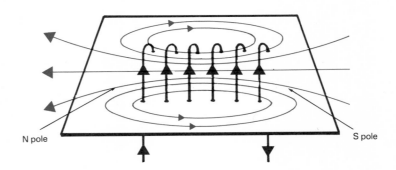

N pole

S pole

Electromagnet

An electromagnet is a solenoid wrapped around a *soft iron* core. The soft iron is magnetised *only* when current flows in the windings. It can thus be switched on and off.

To Increase the Strength of an Electromagnet

1. Increase the number of coil turns.
2. Increase the current.
3. Bring poles closer together (see Horseshoe Electromagnet).

Horseshoe Electro-magnet

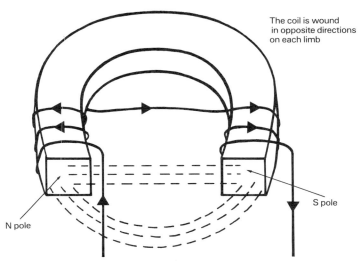

The coil is wound in opposite directions on each limb

S pole

N pole

Some Uses of an Electro-magnet Electric bell; lifting iron objects in a scrapyard; magnetic relays; telephone receivers; motors; loudspeakers.

Microphone A microphone is a device for converting sound energy into electrical energy.

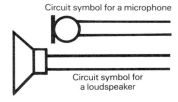

Circuit symbol for a microphone

Loudspeaker A loudspeaker is a device for converting electrical energy into sound energy.

Circuit symbol for a loudspeaker

Magnetic Tape Magnetic tape is a thin strip of plastic, coated with magnetic particles of iron oxide. In unmagnetised tape the particles are randomly distributed and their combined magnetic field is zero.

Tape Head A tape head is a ring-shaped electromagnet with a tiny gap ($\sim 10^{-6}$ m) between its poles. It can:

1. put new audio signals on to a tape (record);
2. pick up audio signals from a tape (playback); and
3. erase a tape.

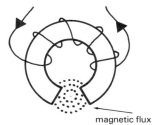

magnetic flux

Recording Audio Signals

Recording audio signals involves a constantly varying (amplified) audio signal producing a constantly varying electric current resulting in a constantly varying magnetic flux. The tape drawn past the poles of the electromagnet is subjected to this magnetic flux which is emitted with a size and polarity proportional to the electrical signal.

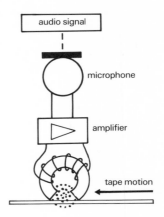

The magnetic particles are aligned in the direction of the magnetising force produced at the time. Degrees of magnetism are produced along the moving tape.

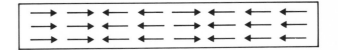

Playback

Playback involves drawing the tape past the airgap of a similar head. The magnetic field variations in the tape induce changing voltages in the coil windings by *electromagnetic induction* (see page 113). These changing voltages correspond to the changing voltages produced originally by the audio signal. A loudspeaker (fed via an amplifier) converts the changing voltages into sound.

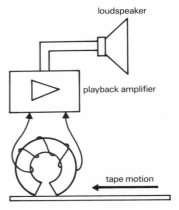

Often the recording and playback functions are performed by the same head.

Erasure

Erasure is carried out by a similar head whose coil windings are fed by radio frequency a.c. The tape is demagnetised and the magnetic particles again become randomly distributed.

Current-Carrying Conductor A current-carrying conductor placed in a magnetic field experiences a force.

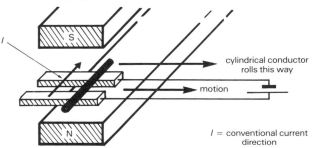

Fleming's Left Hand Rule (F.L.H.R.) If the thumb, first and second fingers of the left hand are held at right angles to each other so that:
the First finger points in the direction of the magnetic Field,
the seCond finger in the direction of conventional Current,
then the thuMb points in the direction of Motion.

The *maximum* force is exerted when the conductor is perpendicular to the magnetic field. The force on a current-carrying straight conductor in a magnetic field is a result of the interaction of its own magnetic field with the one in which it is placed. It increases with increasing field strength and with increasing current.

Current-Carrying Coil A current-carrying coil wrapped around a soft iron cylinder and placed between the concave poles of a permanent magnet experiences a turning effect. If current enters and leaves the coil by springs, it rotates until stopped by the springs.

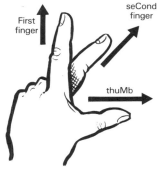

The coil is pivoted in jewelled bearings A and B.

Moving Coil Galvanometer A moving coil galvanometer consists of a current-carrying coil with a pointer attached to it.

Turning Effect of a Current-Carrying Coil in a Magnetic Field

The turning effect of a current-carrying coil in a magnetic field increases with:

1. the strength of the magnetic field;
2. the current;
3. the number of turns on the coil; and
4. weaker hair springs.

Radial Field

A radial field is one where the field lines are directed towards the centre of the cylinder. The concave pole pieces and the soft iron cylinder produce such a field in the air gap.

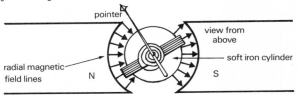

Linear Scale

A linear scale is one where the divisions are the same size. A radial field ensures a linear scale over which the pointer moves.

Springs

The springs determine the angle of rotation of the coil. They enable the coil to return to its original position when the current is switched off. Strong springs allow a coil to rotate through a smaller angle than weak springs.

Simple Electric Motor

A simple electric motor consists of:

1. a coil;
2. a magnetic field; and
3. a split-ring commutator (a split copper ring) against which carbon brushes press.

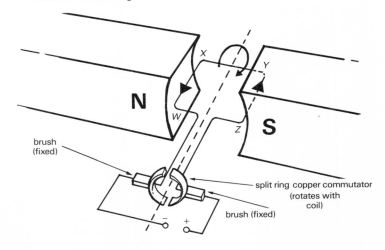

No forces act on *WZ* and *XY* since they are parallel to the field. *WX* experiences an upward force and *YZ* experiences a downward force (apply F.L.H.R). The coil rotates until the commutator halves change contact from one brush to the other. The current through the coil reverses, *WX* now experiences a downward force whilst *YZ* experiences an upward force. The coil rotates clockwise.

Efficiency of a Motor

$$\text{Efficiency of a motor} = \frac{\text{useful mechanical power output}}{\text{electrical power input}}$$

Electro-magnetic Induction

Electromagnetic induction describes the effect of producing electricity from magnetism.

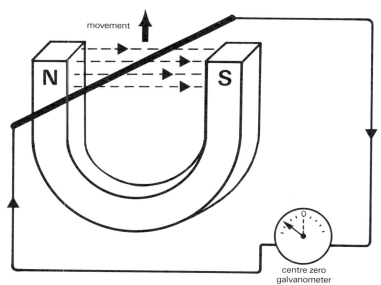

movement

centre zero
galvanometer

A conductor (connected by wires to a galvanometer) is moved in the direction shown between the poles of a permanent magnet. The magnetic lines of flux between the poles are cut. A potential difference is induced between the ends of the conductor. The size of the induced p.d. depends on the rate at which lines of flux are being cut. The greater the rate, the greater the p.d. The induced p.d. depends upon:
1. the length of wire in the field;
2. the strength of the magnetic field; and
3. the speed at which the wire moves.
The p.d. becomes zero when the motion stops. The p.d. results in a tiny current which gives rise to a deflection on the galvanometer.

113

Fleming's Right Hand Rule (F.R.H.R.)

Fleming's Right Hand Rule gives the direction of the induced current for a straight wire moving at right angles to a magnetic field.

If the thumb, first and second fingers of the right hand are held at right angles to each other so that:

the First finger points in the direction of the magnetic Field,

the thuMb in the direction of Motion,

then the seCond finger gives the direction of conventional Current.

Inducing an Electromotive Force (and thus a Current in a Coil)

Inducing an e.m.f. can be achieved by moving a magnet towards or away from the coil. Lines of magnetic flux associated with the magnet are being cut by the turns of the coil.

Fig. 1

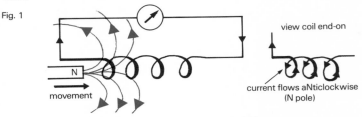

view coil end-on

current flows aNticlockwise (N pole)

Lines of magnetic flux associated with bar magnet

Fig. 2

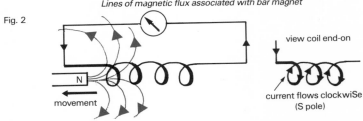

view coil end-on

current flows clockwiSe (S pole)

The direction of the induced current flows in the coil in such a way as to oppose the movement of the magnet. In fig. 1 the turns of the coil take on the appearance of a N pole and in fig. 2 a S pole. If the induced currents caused opposite poles to those that they do, electrical energy would be created from nothing violating the principle of conservation of energy (see page 51).

Direction of the Induced E.M.F.

The direction of the induced e.m.f. is specified by that of the induced current.

Lenz's Law
Lenz's Law states that the induced current always flows in a direction which opposes the change responsible for inducing it.

Size of the Induced E.M.F.
The size of the induced e.m.f. increases if we increase:
1. the rate at which lines of magnetic flux are being cut – increase the speed of the magnet relative to the coil (or vice versa);
2. the area of the coil;
3. the strength of the magnetic field; and
4. the number of coil turns.

Bicycle Dynamo
A bicycle dynamo consists of a magnet on an axle in the vicinity of a stationary coil wrapped around a soft iron core connected to a lamp.

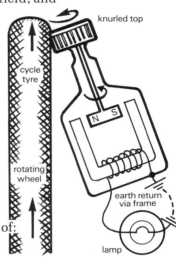

The induced current in the coil makes the lamp light. A faster rotation means that the rate at which lines of magnetic flux are being cut by the coil is increased, resulting in a bigger induced e.m.f. (and current). The lamp becomes brighter.

Simple A.C. Generator
A simple a.c. generator consists of:
1. a coil;
2. a magnetic field; and
3. two slip rings (on the axle of the coil) against which carbon brushes press.

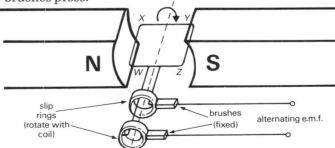

When the coil is rotated it cuts the magnetic field lines. An alternating e.m.f. is induced in the coil. The e.m.f. is a maximum when the coil is horizontal, since *WX* and *YZ* are cutting lines of flux at the greatest rate. When the coil becomes horizontal again, *WX* will be moving downwards and *YZ* upwards. The direction of e.m.f. will reverse.

115

Variation of E.M.F. over One Revolution

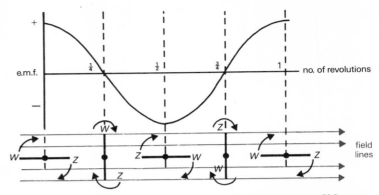

If the coil rotates twenty times per second, the a.c. will have a frequency of 20 Hz.

Mutual Induction

Mutual induction describes the effect of inducing an e.m.f. and current in a coil as a result of switching on, or off, or *changing* a current in a neighbouring coil. Subjecting a coil to a continuously varying magnetic flux pattern is analogous to a coil being cut by lines of magnetic flux as a result of moving a magnet (carrying its own fixed magnetic field pattern) toward or away from it.

The simplest way of doing this is to arrange for an a.c. to run through one of the coils. The magnetic field pattern associated with it will be continuously changing direction. A second coil in the vicinity of the first (preferably wrapped around a common soft iron core to minimise flux leakage) will experience a continuously changing magnetic flux pattern. A continuously changing e.m.f. (and current) will be induced in the second coil.

Transformer

A transformer transforms an alternating e.m.f. from one value to another of greater or smaller value. Primary and secondary coils are wound one on top of the other or on separate limbs of a common soft iron core. An alternating e.m.f. E_p applied to the primary coil induces an alternating e.m.f. E_s in the secondary given by

$$\boxed{\dfrac{E_s}{E_p} = \dfrac{N_s}{N_p}}$$

N_s = number of turns on secondary coil
N_p = number of turns on primary coil

E_p E_s

N_p N_s common soft iron core

Circuit Symbol for a Step-Up Transformer	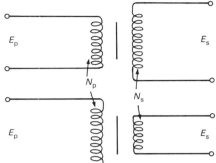	$E_s > E_p$ $N_s > N_p$

| Circuit Symbol for a Step-Down Transformer | | $E_s < E_p$ $N_s < N_p$ |

Transformer Core

The transformer core is made up of sheets of soft iron. Each sheet is insulated from adjacent sheets by varnish which increases the resistance. Heat energy losses inside the iron (a consequence of circulating induced currents inside it called eddy currents) are thus minimised.

Perfect Transformer

The perfect transformer would ensure that all the electrical energy given to the primary appears in the secondary. For a 100% efficient transformer,

Power in primary = power in secondary

i.e.

$$E_p \times I_p = E_s \times I_s$$

where I_p = current in primary, and I_s = current in secondary.

Thus:

$$\frac{E_s}{E_p} = \frac{N_s}{N_p} = \frac{I_p}{I_s}$$

Mains Transformer Hum

Mains transformer hum is a result of its vibrating ferromagnetic core (vibrating bodies provide sound waves). A change in dimensions of ~ 3 parts in 10^5 results from a ferromagnetic substance being magnetised (magnetostriction). For every cycle of a.c., ferromagnetic domains are continually being aligned in one direction and then the other. Since the core has its maximum length when magnetised in either direction, the frequency of the sound waves is 2×50 Hz which is 100 Hz.

Example

If $\dfrac{N_s}{N_p} = 50$, then $\dfrac{I_p}{I_s} = 50$, i.e. $I_s = \left(\dfrac{1}{50}\right) \times I_p$

That is to say, if a step-up transformer has a turns ratio of 50:1, the current is stepped down in the ratio 1:50. Thus the terms step-up and step-down for a transformer refer to E, not I.

117

An Actual Transformer

Because of electrical and magnetic losses, the perfect transformer does not exist. These losses are:

1. eddy currents – it is impossible to eliminate them completely;
2. heat energy produced in the coil windings;
3. the magnetic flux lines produced by the primary may not all cut the secondary – some escape from the core; and
4. hysteresis loss in the magnetic core due to its continued magnetisation and demagnetisation.

Energy Transfer of a Transformer

The energy transfer of a transformer can be over 90% efficient. In calculations we assume a 100% efficiency.

The National Grid

The National Grid transmits power at high voltages (high tension) and low current to minimise power losses in long-distance cabling.

A.C. Power Transmission

Transmission by a.c. enables us to use transformers which *efficiently* step alternating p.d.'s up and down.

U.K. Electricity Distribution System (National Grid)

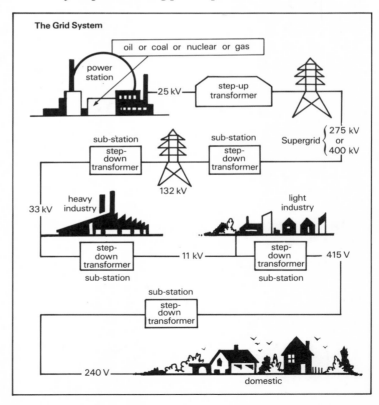

The Grid System

21 The Cathode Ray Oscilloscope

The Oscilloscope

The cathode ray oscilloscope (c.r.o.) is an instrument that allows us to plot graphs of voltage against time on a screen. We 'see' the wave shapes of voltages. It has a very high input resistance (typically 1 MΩ).

Typical C.R.O. Front Panel Layout

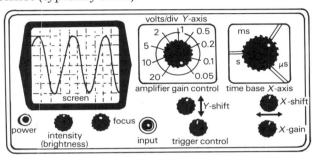

Focus Control

The focus control should be adjusted to give a small clear spot when the c.r.o. is initially switched on.

Brightness Control

The brightness control should not be set too high or the screen will be damaged.

Amplifier Gain Control

The amplifier gain control has a range of fixed gain settings. Each switch position is calibrated in volts per centimetre. The height of the waveform can be measured accurately.

Timebase Control

The timebase control controls the rate at which the spot traverses the screen. Fixed switch positions are calibrated in seconds per centimetre (s/cm), milliseconds per centimetre (ms/cm), or microseconds per centimetre (μs/cm).

Periodic Time (T)

The periodic time is the time for one complete cycle and can be measured using the timebase control.

Frequency of the Waveform (f)

The frequency of the waveform is the reciprocal of the periodic time, i.e. $f = \dfrac{1}{T}$.

Y-Shift Control

The Y-shift control enables the waveform to be moved up or down the screen in the Y direction.

X-Shift Control

The X-shift control enables the waveform to be moved sideways in the X direction.

Trigger Control

The trigger control ensures a steady trace.

Screen

The screen is overlaid with a centimetre grid to allow measurements to be made easily.

Typical C.R.O. Traces
Before an input voltage is applied, the trace is set along the centre grid line.

D.C. Source Voltage
Amplitude gain control set to 3 V/cm. Therefore 6 V d.c.

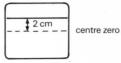

A.C. Source Voltage
Amplitude gain control set to 0.1 V/cm.

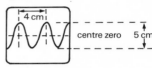

Therefore the peak to peak a.c. voltage is 0.5 V.
(0.1 V/cm × 5 cm).
The peak a.c. voltage is 0.1 V/cm × 2.5 cm = 0.25 V (half the peak to peak voltage). This is the voltage amplitude.

Use of Timebase
Timebase control set to 25 ms/cm. The periodic time for the above a.c. source is the distance in cm between adjacent peaks on a waveform multiplied by the time base control setting:

$$T = 4\,\text{cm} \times \frac{25\,\text{ms}}{\text{cm}} = 100\,\text{ms}.$$

and the frequency of the waveform:

$$f = \frac{1}{T} = \frac{1}{100\,\text{ms}} = \frac{1}{100 \times 10^{-3}\text{s}} = \frac{10^3}{100}\,\text{Hz} = 10\,\text{Hz}$$

C.R.O. Traces which Require Adjustment
Timebase control set too high. Fig. 1

Timebase control set too low. Fig. 2

Amplifier gain set too low. Fig. 3

Amplifier gain set too high. Fig. 4

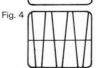

Trigger adjustment required. Fig. 5

22 Electronics

The Potential Divider Circuit

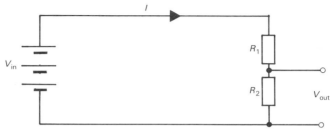

The p.d. across R_1 and R_2, $V_{in} = I(R_1 + R_2)\ldots①$

Also, $V_{out} = IR_2\ldots②$

Potential Divider Equation

$$V_{out} = V_{in}\frac{(R_2)}{(R_1 + R_2)}$$

[Divide equation ② by ① and multiply by V_{in}.]

Example

$$\left.\begin{array}{l} V_{in} = 6\text{ V} \\ R_2 = 100\,\Omega \\ R_1 = 50\,\Omega \end{array}\right\} \Rightarrow V_{out} = 4\text{ V}$$

L.E.D. (Light-Emitting Diode)

A light-emitting diode is a semiconductor diode which converts electrical energy into light. To light up, a p.d. of 2 V across it is needed.

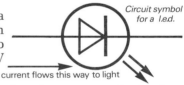

Circuit symbol for a l.e.d.

current flows this way to light

Protective Resistor

A protective resistor is *always* placed in series with a l.e.d. to limit the current through it and the p.d. across it. A p.d. much bigger than 2 V will damage it.

Uses

Uses of l.e.d.'s include:
1. indicator lamps; and
2. seven segment l.e.d. displays in calculators and clocks.

Seven Segment Display

The figure *eight*. All numbers from nought to nine can be made by illuminating different combinations of the seven segments.

L.D.R. (Light Dependent Resistor)

A light-dependent resistor is a resistor whose resistance decreases with increasing light intensity. The more intense the light, the better the l.d.r. conducts electricity.

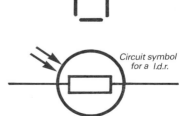

Circuit symbol for a l.d.r.

Thermistor A thermistor is a s.c. whose electrical resistance generally decreases rapidly with increasing temperature. Its resistance can vary from 100 kΩ at room temperature to a few ohms at 100°C.

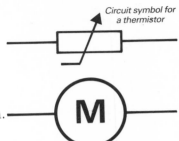

Circuit symbol for a thermistor

Circuit Symbol for a Motor A motor is represented as shown.

Relay A relay is an electromagnetic switch. A small current in one circuit operates a switch (via an electromagnet) in a second circuit. The second circuit often carries a much larger current.

Switching a Motor on via a Relay

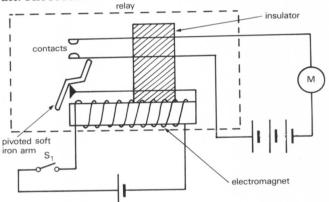

Operation
1. Close S_1.
2. Electromagnet energises.
3. Soft iron arm (called an armature) is pulled towards electromagnet.
4. Contacts close.
5. Current flows through motor.

Circuit Symbol for a Normally Open or Normally Closed Relay

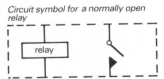

Circuit symbol for a normally open relay

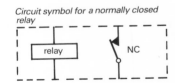

Circuit symbol for a normally closed relay

Transducer A transducer is a device for converting a non-electrical quantity (e.g. light, heat, sound) into electrical signals. Examples include l.d.r.'s, thermistors and microphones.

Transistor A transistor is a current amplifying device. It is often used as a high-speed switch.

NPN Transistor

An npn transistor has three terminals:
c = collector
b = base
e = emitter

Transistor as a Switch

OFF when no collector current flows.
ON when sufficient collector current flows to give a small collector-emitter voltage.
A minimum base-emitter voltage of about 0.6 V is necessary.

Switching on a Transistor Using a Potential Divider

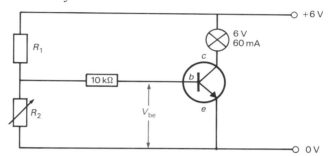

The base-emitter voltage V_{be} is the p.d. across R_2 (variable). This depends on the resistance of R_2 compared with R_1. When $V_{be} > 0.6$ V the transistor switches on and the lamp lights. A very small base-emitter current allows a much larger collector-emitter current to flow. The 10 kΩ resistor ensures only a small current is allowed to flow into the base.

Light-Dependent Switch

(i) Indicator Lamp On in the Dark

The light level sensitivity control is R_1.

R_1 dictates how dark it needs to be before the indicator lamp switches on.
The 2.2 kΩ protective resistor ensures that should R_1 ever tend to zero, the current through the transistor will still be low. If the l.d.r. is covered its resistance is high and V_{be} is high enough for the transistor to switch on. The lamp lights. Varying R_1 changes V_{be}.

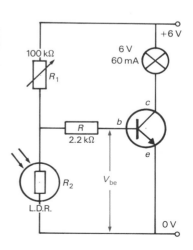

123

(ii) Indicator Lamp Off in the Dark

> The light level sensitivity control is R_2.

R_2 dictates how dark it needs to be before the indicator lamp switches off.
If light is incident on the l.d.r. its resistance drops and V_{be} is high enough for the transistor to switch on. The lamp lights.
Covering the l.d.r. results in a high R_1 (compared to R_2). The transistor switches off and the lamp goes out.
Varying R_2 changes V_{be}.

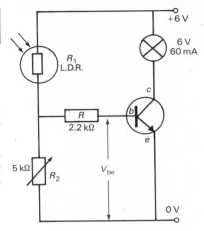

Temperature-Dependent Switch

(i) Indicator Lamp on in the Cold

> The light level sensitivity control is R_1.

R_1 dictates how cold it needs to get before the indicator lamp switches on.
As the thermistor gets colder its resistance increases, so its share of the 6 V increases and the transistor switches on. The lamp lights.

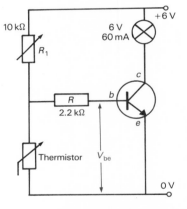

(ii) Indicator Lamp Off in the Cold

> The light level sensitivity control is R_2.

R_2 dictates how cold it needs to get before the indicator lamp switches off.
As the thermistor gets hotter its resistance decreases and its share of the 6 V decreases. V_{be} increases until the transistor switches on. The lamp lights.

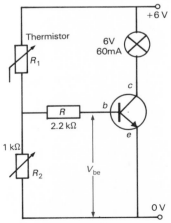

Light-Dependent Switch Operated by a Relay

Lamp On in the Dark

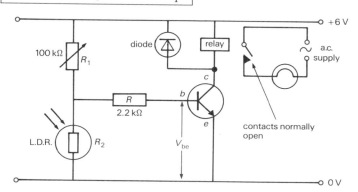

The sensitivity control is R_1

The darker it gets the bigger the resistance of the l.d.r. and the bigger its share of the 6 V. V_{be} increases. The transistor switches on. The relay* switches on. The contacts close. The lamp lights. R_1 dictates how dark it needs to get before the lamp lights.

*A *reverse biased* diode is connected in parallel with the relay to divert current away from the transistor when the relay is switched off. Switching off the relay results in lines of magnetic flux collapsing in a very short time. This gives rise to a large e.m.f. induced in the coil of the relay. The e.m.f. gives rise to a current which could destroy the transistor.

Logic Circuits

Logic circuits use electrical signals for inputs and outputs.

Logic Gates

Logic gates can be either OFF or ON.

Logic 0

Logic 0 stands for OFF. It corresponds to an input p.d. of 0 Volts.

Logic 1

Logic 1 stands for ON. It corresponds to an input p.d. > 0 Volts.

T.-T.L. Levels

Transistor-Transistor Logic Levels. Logic 0 is < 0.4 V. Logic 1 is between 2.4 V and 5 V.   0.4 V to 2.4 V is avoided.

Truth Table for an AND Gate

inputs

A	B	output
0	0	0
0	1	0
1	0	0
1	1	1

circuit symbol

input *A*
input *B*
AND
output

The output is ON (Logic 1) only when both input *A* AND input *B* are ON.

125

Truth Table for a NOT Gate

input	output
0	1
1	0

A **NOT** gate is an *inverter*. The output is the opposite of the input.

circuit symbol

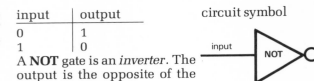

Truth Table for an OR Gate

inputs		output
A	B	output
0	0	0
0	1	1
1	0	1
1	1	1

The output is ON (Logic 1) when either or both inputs *A* and *B* are ON.

circuit symbol

Combining an AND Gate with a NOT Gate

Output of **AND** gate is input to **NOT** gate. This combination can be replaced by a single gate known as a **NAND** gate.

Truth Table for a NAND Gate

inputs		output
A	B	output
0	0	1
0	1	1
1	0	1
1	1	0

circuit symbol

Combining an OR Gate with a NOT Gate

Output of **OR** gate is input to **NOT** gate. This combination can be replaced by a single gate known as a **NOR** gate.

Truth Table for a NOR Gate	inputs			
	A	B	output	
	0	0	1	
	0	1	0	
	1	0	0	
	1	1	0	

circuit symbol

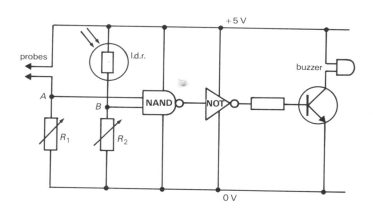

Logic Gate Application

Students should appreciate that logic gates require:
1. a power supply input; and
2. an earth or return line.

Circuit for Detecting Moisture in Daylight

R_1 = moisture sensitivity control
R_2 = light level sensitivity control

For the buzzer to 'buzz' we require (working backwards):
1. the output from the **NOT** gate to be a logical 1;
2. the input to the **NOT** gate to be a logical 0 (see Truth Table for **NOT** gate);
3. the output from the **NAND** gate to be a logical 0;
4. the two inputs to the **NAND** gate to be logical 1 (see Truth Table for **NAND** gate);
5. the resistance of the l.d.r. to be low for the potential at B to be high. (We want most of the voltage drop to be across R_2.) The resistance of a l.d.r. decreases with increasing light intensity, so we want DAYLIGHT;
6. the resistance between the detector probes to be low for the potential at A to be high. (We want most of the voltage drop across R_1.) Hence the detector probes should be moist.

N.B. The **NAND** gate followed by the **NOT** gate in the above circuit could be replaced with an **AND** gate.

Index